WEARABLE DREAMS

OUT OF AFRICA

Wearable dreams brings to us a wealth of inspiration and technique in these creative and 'soulful' garments. They are timeless fashion... sculptural artforms.

Photographic detail, colour and self explanatory notes make the techniques used in the construction of these garments easily understood. This is fabric manipulation at its best.

This creative clothing transcends fashion and moves these techniques into the realm of fibre art and décor.

FRONT COVER: Detail from "The Guardian" – Jutta Faulds (page 40)

BACK COVER: Detail of waistcoat – Sue Akerman

TITLE PAGE: Detail of "Sunbird" by Jutta Faulds (pages 52/55)

First Published 1999

PUBLISHED BY   **NORTH AMERICAN DISTRIBUTOR**

Triple T Publishing c.c.   Quilters Resources inc.

29 Colenso Road   P.O. Box 148850

Claremont 7700   Chicago IL, 60614

Cape Town, South Africa   U.S.A.

PHOTOGRAPHY:

Lesley Turpin-Delport   Barry Downard   Ivan van den Boogaard

MODELS:

Ilva Lawrence   Nicola Walsh   Philip Delport

Mandy Ross-MacDonald   Ivan van den Boogaard   Jennifer Mbewu

Sarah Akerman   Lucy Grant   Kate Grant

Sonja Poule

Typesetting & Repro: Fotoplate, Cape Town

Printed by: Mills Litho, Cape Town

COPYRIGHT © TRIPLE T PUBLISHING 1999

ISBN 0-958-4227-1-0

OTHER BOOKS PUBLISHED BY TRIPLE T PUBLISHING

SATIN & SILK RIBBON EMBROIDERY
by Lesley Turpin-Delport
ISBN 0-620-17755-1

JUST FLOWERS
by Lesley Turpin-Delport
ISBN-0-958-3873-3-8

JUST DESIGNS
by Lesley Turpin-Delport
ISBN 0-958 3873-6-2

TWO CUSHIONS AND A QUILT
by Sue Akerman
ISBN 0-958-3873-1-1

THE LIBERATED CANVAS
by Penny Cornell
ISBN 0-958-3873-4-6

LET'S SMOCK IT
by Patricia Muñoz Timmins
ISBN 0-958-3873-8-9

QUILTS ON SAFARI
by Jenny Williamson & Pat Parker
ISBN 0-958-3873-9-7

About the Author

Sue is a born and bred African. Her first love for patchwork was kindled when she visited an Amish community in the United States of America as an exchange student.

Since then she has grown immensely in her own work, always breaking new ground, challenging norms and dreaming up new creations.

Sue uses her work to make a statement. Her work carries a message, has a soul of its own, and is not merely the rich surface the eye sees. She draws a huge amount of inspiration from nature and her surroundings. Sue considers herself a contemporary quilt maker, dreaming up wearable and wall quilts – embellishment and embroidery being her great loves.

A major change in her wearable art career came when she was invited to participate in the Fairfield fashion show. Since then she has subsequently made another 3 garments for their travelling exhibitions. Her clothing is made to be worn by beings as well as by walls. Sue has made these works of art versatile so that they can be enjoyed at all times, texture and colour being her uppermost priorities. She loves nothing more than to be drawn to a piece of work because it says "touch me".

Sue is the author of an embroidery book "Two Cushions and a Quilt". She has taught and exhibited both nationally and internationally and is always willing to share every last morsel of information at her fingertips.

INSPIRATION THAT INSPIRES ME TO GREATER HEIGHTS

These words hang on my sewing room walls

Only as high as we reach –
Can we grow;
Only as far as we seek –
Can we go;
Only as deep as we look –
Can we see;
Only as much as we dream –
Can we be.

I dedicate this book to ...

My friends who inspire me and who have created these wonderful garments. For their willingness to share them with the world. Without them this book would not have been as diverse nor as exciting.

They are: Jutta Faulds, Sally Scott, Nina Lawrence, Betty Beekes, Marge Gatter, Sue Funston and Annette MacMaster.

My husband Hugh, my support and the best friend I could ever wish for, and my children Gareth, Mark and Sarah-Jane. Thank you for allowing me the time to enable this dream to become a reality.

Lastly, to my Creator for my talents and showing me a way to share them.

Acknowledgement

Mike Tripp and Lesley Turpin-Delport of Triple T Publishing, thank you for sharing in my dream and believing that it was worth realizing.

My gratitude also goes to Barry Downard and Ivan van den Boogaard who also came to my rescue with their amazing photographic talents.

INDEX

WARDROBE

TECHNIQUES

Foreword

The very thought of Africa conjures up an aura of mystery, diversity, excitement and beauty. This is the heart of where this work comes from. In much of the work the beauty of Africa's soul is evident. The artists have worked with adventurous spirits, with no tradition to follow and a strong desire to create. They have had to be innovative and daring, always breaking rules and boundaries, constantly challenging the norms of western clothing.

The wide open spaces, the smell of the first rains in the bushveld, the sunsets saturated in colour, the diversity of the people and their culture, the wildlife and closeness to nature are all an abundance of inspiration.

The reason for writing this book is to share these garments as they are a testimony to the unique country that we live in. This is a truly African experience of African creativity.

It has a feel of its own and if this is not enough come and see for yourself!

It is from a country of vastly contrasting lifestyles and little inheritance of "Art clothing" other than the tribal dress of our ancestors that these garments have been born.

Enjoy the inspiration and the celebration of creative clothing. I hope that you too will be moved to produce your own totally unique garment once having read this book.

Right: FREEDOM FLIGHT – *Back detail*
This section of the garment can be unbuttoned and worn as a neck piece – this versatility allows maximum use. Beading, machine embroidery and shisha mirrors are all used and make it "work" when worn on its own.

Opposite page: FREEDOM FLIGHT
Was made at a time when South Africa was undergoing great political change – like a moth being set free so this country was about to be liberated. A combination of seductive taffetas, fine chiffon and cotton fabrics were used in its construction (see page 41 backview; 43 detail).

What is Wearable Art?
and What is Wearable?

What is wearable art?

I once heard it described as "TIMELESS FASHION – A SCULPTURAL ARTFORM". It never dates as true fashion trends do, but because of its truly artistic nature, lives on forever. It is tactile and visually pleasing.

What is wearable?

Anything is wearable! This depends entirely on the wearer of the garment and for what purpose it is being worn. The old adage of "one man's meat is another man's poison" really pertains to clothing, and what each individual chooses to wear.

I guess that the answer to this question is, that if the art piece is wearable, it is made specifically to relate to the human form as well as providing some sort of covering, that being for protection, warmth, or purely to make an artistic statement about the wearer or the clothing on a body.

This book is not intended to take you step by step through a project so that you all end up with a similar looking garment. It is rather to inspire you with wonderful ideas and give you direction as to how to achieve your own creative ideas.

I really hope that this book will be an encouragement to those already inspired, as well as provide a host of technical information for those who are beginning their creative journey and need to get started.

Should you need to know "How to?" I have dedicated a section to technique.

I'm sure that the photos will saturate the appetite of everyone else.

These clothes are a whole new experience to make and wear. They become conversation pieces, and my advice to you is:

MAKE THEM, WEAR THEM, and most of all SHARE THEM!

The Creative Spirit

To "Create", as defined in a dictionary, means to produce or make something. For me creating means more than that. To be truly creative, I believe, is to have the ability to put your own stamp on your work making it totally unique. Being a great technician does not necessarily mean that you are creating to your best potential. A creation is the product of your own choices and interpretations. It is incredibly important to be true to your own creative spirit – copying is not creative, it is being technically efficient.

I would like to challenge you all to make a piece of work from your own soul and not someone else's. If this sounds too terrifying then don't leap, just try small steps at a time and you will witness your work growing in leaps and bounds, as you develop your own style of working and your work grows in character.

Carl Sandberg once wrote: 'NOTHING HAPPENS UNLESS FIRST A DREAM'.

Dreaming is a good place to begin. These garments are an emotional, personal and creative part of the designer's soul. They are often a reflection of the maker at a given point in their artistic career, either creatively or emotionally.

How many of you have said, "I wish I could do that!". YOU CAN. Get started, "Live now, believe me, wait not till tomorrow, gather the roses of life today". Life can be precious and time short, so don't waste any more. Creativity is the act of transferring a vision in one's mind into an actual happening. Creativity is also playful and cannot be pre-planned. It is a growing process. I have often likened the creative process to a journey. There is a starting point and an end, and in-between things don't always go according to plan. Sometimes you have to change your route quite radically. How you get to the end of the journey does not count, the only thing that matters is the end result. A long road and hours of hands on working, enhances the whole process. In order to create something one needs a point of departure. Dream, then Design and lastly Do it. The three D's in the creative process:

DREAMING

This is the easy part, especially when we are surrounded by inspiration and you are aware of the inspiration. Some people never realise just what is at their fingertips because they have not learned to see. Develop a Seeing Eye. Carry a notebook with you always, in which you can jot down ideas and sketches.

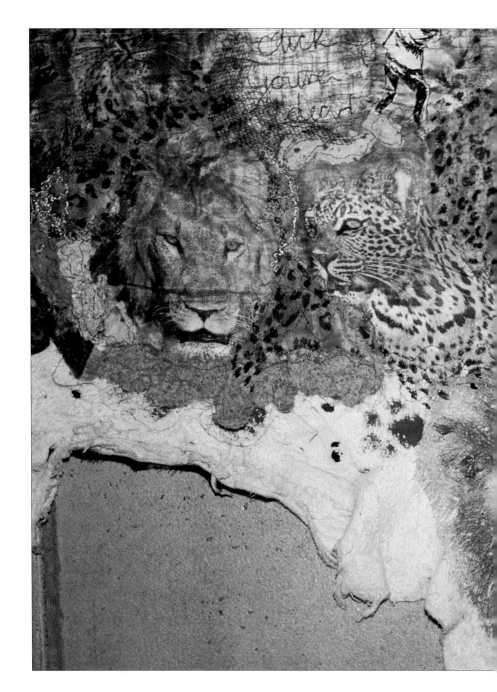

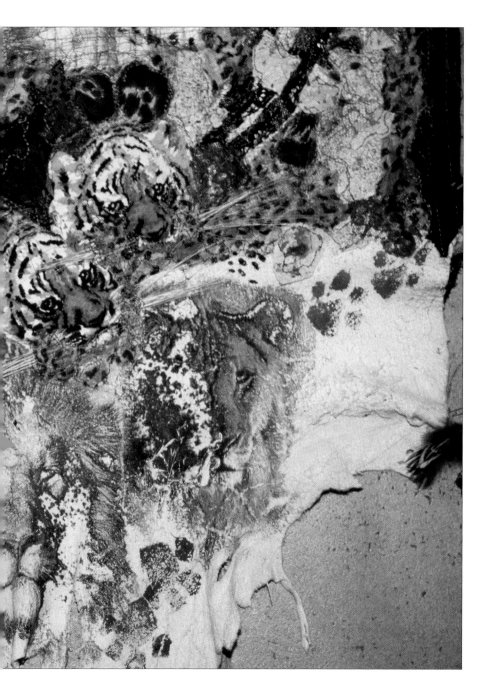

DESIGN AND DRAWING

I always make a rough sketch of what I want to do and use this as a point of departure. Never limit yourself with ideas, as they may change as the piece of work grows. Sometimes it helps to put fabrics together and look at them day after day. This helps with colour choice. Give yourself time so that all your ideas can gel.

DOING

Once you start a project your creative juices will begin to flow. Forget about what others might do or say, trust your own intuition and inner soul.

FEEDING YOUR CREATIVE SOUL

- Be in touch with nature and your surroundings. Paul Cezanne once wrote, "the day is coming when a single carrot freshly observed will set off a revolution."
- Expose yourself to other art and craft forms as they are all inter-related.
- Attend courses that you might not regularly or ordinarily attend.
- Keep your eyes WIDE open and develop a Seeing Eye.
- Carry a notebook with you. An ideas book.
- Allow yourself time to be creative.
- Push yourself to your maximum. Don't run before you can crawl, but continuously challenge yourself.
- Use materials, colours or techniques that you wouldn't normally use with every new project.
- Be gently critical of your own work. Try not to be over critical.
- Ask colleagues, whose ability and advice you respect to critique your work.
- Experiment.

If I can make a final analogy: the creative journey is like gathering a bouquet of flowers. The starting point is picking the first flower and then one by one adding to it. Some may need to be discarded due to their colour or shape, you may need to add more of others, at the end you will have a beautiful creation in your hands.

Left: Detail from – FRIEND OR FOE – (Sue Akerman)
A heavily machine embellished piece using photocopy transfers. This was a statement on "Canned Hunting" and my disgust for this cowardly "sport" – for photocopy transfer technique see page 24.

Tactile Texture

Amazing textural surfaces can be created with fabric because of the very nature of its makeup. This will also depend on just how much or how little the specific fabric will allow. i.e. thickness, fineness, weight and pliability of the fabric.

The following chapters are dedicated to the techniques of texturing and manipulating fabric and thread, resulting in exciting fibre changes.

My only advice would be to experiment, experiment, experiment. Through experimentation one often stumbles upon or discovers wonderful new ways of doing things, as well as surprises. I have often found easier ways of designing through experimentation.

Remember to try all the options that come to mind. There are hundreds of them and I think that we probably all wish that we had more time for experimentation. In fact sometimes its good to just play rather than make a specific project.

Try doing things in a different way.

Cut holes in the fabric; fray it; burn it; pleat it; rouch it; paint it; scrunch and sew it; cut it on the bias; cut strips and top stitch; embroider it; quilt it. There are many permutations.

Texture in general refers to the surface effect. The tactile nature of some kinds of fabric surface invite the viewer to touch and look closer at it. Textures in landscape surround us, and by looking and touching one can begin to understand the very nature of them. Think of bark or weathered rocks, one is automatically compelled to touch or feel them, or just look closer.

I'm sure this is why I love the tactile nature of fabric and thread. When making garments it is incredibly important to have quiet as well as textured areas. The garment can very easily become overworked if too textured. At the same time it can run the risk of being boring if left plain or by using the same type of overall effect.

Right: "Creative juices" flow when you open your eyes to your surroundings.

Fabulous Fabrics

Most of us have chosen to use fabric as our artistic medium because of its tactile nature, incredible richness and manipulative properties. Fabric artists are usually incredible hoarders of fabric. I'm sure everyone's stash of fabrics looks totally different, according to locality and taste. A very good habit to get into is to pre-wash all fabrics before they find a spot on your shelf with all the other fabrics. In this way you will always know that everything has been washed and ready for use.

In South Africa we do not have huge patchwork stores with rows of 100% cotton fabrics to choose from. Instead we have exotic Indian retailers who stock elaborate, vibrant, shiny, seductive fabrics, wonderful on one hand but disastrous on the other as these fabrics do everything that you don't want a fabric to do. They can be very difficult to piece together. They slip and slide all over the place and unravel. These fabrics can be stabilised by ironing vialene onto the back. We do have cottons available but often find it easier to resort to dying fabric.

When stitching so many different kinds of fabrics together it is more difficult to care for the finished item. Unequal shrinkage and stretch can be a problem. Extra care must be taken when laundering these garments.

Remember to use the correct needles on your machine for the different fabrics. Blunt needles can make holes in fine or stretch fabrics. Change the machine needle regularly.

Never throw any scraps away as they can be used for machine embroidery. When I complete a garment or a quilt I put all the scraps and slivers into a see through plastic bag and store them in a bigger bag all together. In this way when doing network appliqué or embroidery, half the work is done as you have onhand a whole range of blended scraps to work with.

The use of different types of fabric has lead to the vibrancy in the garments in this book.

Left: Never be afraid of the textile composition of fabric. A small amount of a very rich fabric can enhance a garment.

Colour

Colour is the sensation produced by the effect of light waves striking the retina of the eye. It is no wonder that the colour of a garment has the ability to change the whole feel and character of the piece.

Light and **bright** colours in a garment will make areas advance or make the whole garment more noticeable. They can also add weight to an individual wearing them. They often radiate a feeling of happiness, well-being and self-confidence.

Dark, dull coloured garments tend to recede and give lightness to the wearer.

Warm colours advance (Red, yellow etc.)

Cool colours recede (blues, greens).

Monochromatic colour schemes are restful but can run the risk of becoming boring. Use texture in these garments to give a lift to the colour scheme. A small amount of a shiny surface here and there will enhance the surrounding colours i.e. silk.

Complementary colours can be used when a dramatic effect is required. (These are opposite on the colour wheel.)

The more one works with colour the more confident you will feel about using different combinations.

Experiment with colours that you don't normally use, these are often very rewarding challenges. Do not be afraid of breaking rules and taking risks as these often result in exciting new discoveries.

Remember that the more colours used, the busier a garment will look.

Harmony is often created by colour repetition. A small amount of a strong colour, for example, yellow, can be so strong in its own right that it distracts the viewer from the whole piece. You may need to add more of this strong colour in order to offset or balance it.

We all seem to favour different colours. I may love red and orange while you may find them hot and uncomfortable. One colour may have a calming effect on you but to someone else it may have a depressive effect.

Try not to stick to using your tried and tested favourites but rather experience growth in your work by experimenting with new colours.

Buy or make yourself a colour wheel to hang on the wall of your sewing room or studio. One can never stop learning about colour and its interaction, so take time out to attend courses and experiment on your own.

The colour wheel and all its possibilities can spark off new inspiration.

African Inspiration

Just to complete the introduction to garments which follow, here are some inspirational ideas, out of Africa. You can find them in your environment.

The mystery behind African masks and beautifully executed Tribal baskets and cloth all give us food for thought.

In the winter when the thatch grass by the roadside is long – the dust hangs in the crisp air – the early morning sun melts the dew and warms the frosted ground. Africa comes alive and feeds our souls.

Right: BUSHVELD INFLUENCES – (Sue Akerman)

Below: MAD CATS – CHILD'S WAISTCOAT – (Sue Akerman) – *(See page 16).*

Left: DESERT ELEGANCE – (Sue Akerman)

Left: WAISTCOAT FOR ALL OCCASIONS – (Nina Lawrence)

Right: CHAIN MAIL VEST – (Sue Akerman)

Left: EMBROIDERED WAISTCOAT –
(Sue Akerman)

ROUND PEGS IN SQUARE HOLES – (Sue Akerman)

Above, left: Symmetry can make a garment predictable. Always try and create something unexpected making it more interesting.

Above, right: GOLDFISH WAISTCOAT – (Sue Akerman) – *(See page 16).*

LAYERED WAISTCOAT –
(Sue Akerman) – *(See page 19).*

Network Appliqué

TROPICAL FISH WAISTCOATS

Network Appliqué is the laying down of many scraps of fabric onto a background material and securing them in place with a layer of net and machine stitching.

In order to make a garment of this nature, one needs to decide on the theme for the embroidery. For this project we will use fantasy tropical fish.

1) Cut your two basic waistcoat pattern fronts out of a background fabric.
2) Cut two identical size pieces of double-sided vilene and lay them on top of the background fabric.
3) Scatter small scraps of fabric over the two waistcoat fronts and vilene. Remember to concentrate the richest colours where the accent images are to be formed. The scraps of fabric do not need to be laid in the exact shape of the fish (or image) but should occupy the general area. Only a small overlap of the scraps is permissible as they must be in contact with the vilene.
4) Secure the pieces in position by ironing them with a hot iron.
5) Place a piece of net over the entire piece of fabric and scraps.
6) Prepare your machine by dropping the feed dog and moving the stitch setting in a straight stitch position – use the darning foot attachment.
7) Using contrast threads on your machine, embroider the fish.
   A machine embroidery hoop can be used if required – refer to the machine embroidery section for technique. You may want to use one of the fish diagrams as an inspiration, and transfer it onto your waistcoat with a chalk pencil or marking pen. Imagine that you are drawing with your machine, but instead of having a pen and paper in hand, you have a thread and needle. Use as many colours of thread as you desire. The background areas will also need to be secured with meandering stitchery.

SPECIAL EFFECTS

Add hand embroidery to the accent areas.

Try overlapping different colours of net as this creates exciting colour changes.

Above: MAD CATS – (Sue Akerman)
Buttons add to the naive feel of this child's waistcoat. Variegated embroidery threads cut down work, and create exciting colour changes in the stitching.

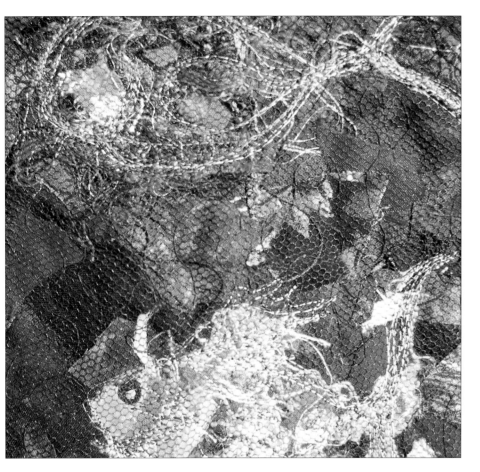

WAISTCOAT ASSEMBLY

1) Cut two pattern fronts and one back out of lining fabric.
2) Cut one back out of background fabric.
3) Stitch the back and front lining sections together at the shoulders.
4) Stitch the front and back sections together at the shoulders. Press the seams flat.
5) With the right sides together, pin the lining to the garment, making sure that the centre backs and seams match. Stitch the lower front, fronts and neck edges.
6) Stitch the armhole edges and lower back opening together. Leave the 2 side seams open.
7) Trim and clip the seams.
8) Turn the lining to the inside by pulling the front sections through the shoulders and both out of one of the side openings in the back.
9) Press.
10) Stitch the fronts to the back, and the front lining to the back at the sides in one continuous seam.
11) Slip stitch the two openings at the side seams.
12) Wear it!

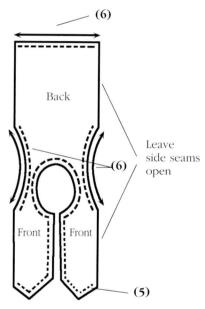

The end result.

(2) Lay the vilene on top of the background fabric.

(3) Lay the scraps of fabric on top of the background fabric and vilene.

(5) Place a piece of net over the scraps. Then iron it.

(7) Add detail with machine embroidery.

Rouching / Crinkled Fabric

1. When texturing fabric in this way, take a piece of fabric in your hands and pleat it. (The fabric will obviously crease better if it is a natural fibre)
2. Twist it tightly so that it folds back on itself.
3. Use elastic bands to hold the twists in place.
4. Wet the fabric thoroughly and then squeeze out any excess water.
5. Leave this in the sun or tumble dry. Drying will take approximately 3 hours in a tumble dryer.
6. When it is dry, unwrap the fabric.
7. Lay a piece of vilene down onto a flat surface, sticky side up, and place your crinkled fabric on top of it. Make sure that all the pleats and folds are as you want them. Maintain all the crinkles and wrinkles in the fabric created with the twisting process.
8. Iron the fabric to the vilene using a hot iron. This will stabilise the fabric and keep the wrinkles in place.

SPECIAL EFFECTS

- With a straight stitch setting on your machine stitch between the hills and the valleys of the crinkles.
- Some of the wrinkles may be big enough to slip a piece of piping or fabric underneath. This can then be stitched down creating an accent or focal point.
- Contrasting threads and topstitching can also be very effective using a double needle.
- Create areas of intricate detail, by sewing beads and working hand or machine embroidery into some of the pleats.

ROUCHING FABRIC USING SHIRRING ELASTIC

When using this method of rouching fabric, do remember that because you are using elastic to pull up the fabric, there will be a lot of instability of the fabric. You may elect to stabilise the fabric onto vilene once it has all been drawn up.

Use a large piece of fabric, as its size will decrease dramatically with the rouching. Remember that the heavier the weight of the fabric the less it will gather and the lighter the fabric the more it will gather.

Hand wind shirring [hat] elastic onto a bobbin.

Using a zigzag stitch, lines can be stitched parallel; criss-crossing one another or simply using a random pattern.

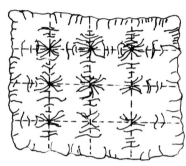

Rouching with shirring elastic or tacking.

SPECIAL EFFECTS

Strips of fabric can be cut and their raw edges stitched under and then shirring elastic stitched down either side. These rouched strips work very well when a tricky area is needed to be joined. In this way one can top stitch one of these strips over the raw edges that otherwise might have been visible.

Fabric can also be gathered or rouched by sewing parallel lines of running stitches and then individually drawing them up as required.

Layered Fabrics

Note the difference in effect, cutting the fabric on the straight grain or on the bias.

Layering fabrics and then cutting into them to discover what is underneath can be extremely exciting. 100% cotton fabrics work the best for this method of piecing. Most machines can cope with four layers of fabric. More layers can be stitched together if a stronger needle is used.

To make a waistcoat with this method cut 4 different fabrics for each piece of the garment. These fabrics must be cut slightly bigger than the pattern pieces. The top layer will be the most dominant and this should be the fabric that you want to be most visible.

The bottom layer will be the least visible and will form the lining.

The 2 middle layers should be of a good contrast, as only their ruffled edges will show.

Pin these 4 layers together.

You can draw your own pattern onto the top surface and sew along these lines or you can stick to vertical, horizontal or diagonal lines.

METHOD

Using a straight machine stitch, length 3, sew parallel lines about $^1/_4$ inch / $^3/_4$ cm. apart. DO NOT STITCH ACROSS ANY LINES. These parallel lines create channels over the entire surface.

Stitching across the bias of the fabric will give a more ravelled effect. Stitching with the straight grain of the fabric will give a less ravelled effect.

Using small, very sharp scissors cut through the top THREE layers of fabric leaving the bottom layer intact.

Pop the fabric into the washing machine. Any abrasive action helps with the unravelling.

Spin the fabric, and dry in the tumble dryer. Any other clothes like jeans are good to put into the tumble drier with these pieces of fabric. This abrasive action helps the fabric unravel.

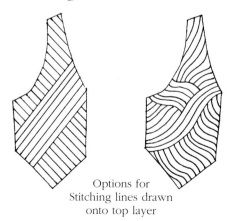

Options for Stitching lines drawn onto top layer

Layered Fabrics *(continued)*

DIAGONALLY STITCHED OPTION

1. Cut 4 squares of fabric all the same size. Use 4 different fabrics.
2. Draw a grid of diagonal lines 1 – 2 inches (2.5 – 5 cm) apart with a marking pen on the top layer of fabric.
3. Layer the top 3 fabrics and pin them together. Leave the base piece of fabric out of this sandwich.
4. Sew straight stitching lines on the grid that has been drawn.
5. Place the three pieces of fabric that have been stitched together onto the cutting board and with a rotary cutter and ruler cut through all the layers from corner to corner of each block. Being very careful not to cut the stitching lines.

Once this has been done, place this piece onto the base piece and re-stitch all the grid lines that were drawn on the top piece, thus joining all four pieces together.

Wash and dry as explained in the previous section.

Join the garment pieces together. Cover all the unfinished seams with a binding. Bind the edge of the garment with a contrast or like coloured binding in order to finish it off.

SPECIAL EFFECTS

- Spectacular results can be achieved by merely placing different fabrics one on top of the other, stitching them down and then cutting into them to find underlying colour.
- Try using numerous fabrics sewn together to form a base layer, rather than just one. Make these quite a strong contrast.

 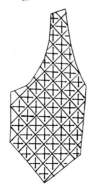

2. Draw a grid of diagonal lines and, using these lines as a guide, stitch through the top 3 layers of fabric.

5. The +'s indicate where to cut through the top layers of fabric.

Tucks and Pleats

There are numerous ways of creating tucks and pleats in fabric and in this way creating wonderful textural effects. Any fabric that can be creased or folded can be used, although one must remember that in this way you are adding bulk to fabric so the best fabrics to use are really those that are thinner but also have stability. By this I mean fabrics that are able to hold their shape. Striped fabrics can look wonderful when tucked and are easily worked as the striped pattern can be used as the stitching guide.

Movement is created when tucks are twisted and sewn down in different directions.

Remember that fabric size is reduced when making tucks and pleats, so work them before cutting out the pattern pieces.

Pintucks

Pin tucks are very narrow ridges of fabric created by sewing with a double needle.

Pin tucks are sewn on the machine by inserting a double needle into your machine and threading the machine with 2 reels of cotton. Thicker ridges can be created by working with cord or wool underneath the fabric and stitching over the top of it. This cord is threaded up through the hole in the needle plate of the machine, and pulled to the back of the presser foot before commencing stitching.

Pin tucks can be sewn in parallel lines, criss-crossing each other or in wavy patterns.

Contrast or metallic threads can be used for special effects.

It is often a good idea, to pin tuck a large area of fabric and then cut it up as required.

Mark the first line where pin tucks are to be stitched, and stitch on this line. The presser foot can now be used as a guide for the following rows. When stitching the next row, allow the foot to run up against the last line of pin tucks that has already been sewn.

A myriad of techniques were used in this waistcoat construction. The colours pull it together.

This collar is buttoned on to the waistcoat and can be removed. Slivers of fabric and thread have been trapped under the net and topstitched into place.

Left: SKIRT – (Sally Scott)
Note the effective use of contrast top stitching.

Flat Tucks

Flat tucks are bigger tucks than pin tucks, and can be made as wide or narrow as required, depending on the effect desired. They create wonderful light and dark values, because of their 3 dimensional nature. It is often a good idea to tuck a large piece of fabric and then cut it into pieces.

METHOD.

1. With a marking pen or pencil and grid ruler draw parallel lines onto your fabric 1¹/₂" / 4cm apart. (These become the folding lines). This width obviously differs according to the effect that is required. Draw all the lines before you begin stitching.
2. Fold the fabric on the first line drawn. Set the needle position to the furthest setting on the left.
3. With the right side of your machine foot on that fold of the fabric and the bulk of the fabric out to the left of the machine, begin stitching. Sew a straight line along the entire width of the fabric. Thus creating the first pleat.
4. Fold the fabric on the next drawn line and continue until the entire piece has been pleated.
5. Using a steam iron, press all the pleats in one direction.

TO CREATE A FEELING OF MOVEMENT — TWIST THE PLEATS

Stitch the pleats down on either side, not less than 4" / 10cm apart, stitching the pleats in the same direction.

Now stitch straight up the centre in the opposite direction, forcing the pleats to flip up and lie in the opposite direction.

Another option is to stitch them down on one side in one direction and on the other side in the opposite direction.

SPECIAL EFFECTS

As in diagram 2, use a machine embroidery stitch or contrast cotton to stitch up the centre of the pleats.

To stabilise the tucks embellish them with machine or hand embroidery stitches.

Stabilise the tucks by stitching them down in different directions.

Using a plain white or cream cotton fabric, flat tuck an entire piece. Stitch the tucks down in different directions and colour them with fabric paints. Paint one colour on the underside of the tuck, and another on the upper side of the tuck. They will bleed into each other a little, but this will create interesting effects.

Smocking Pleats

A smocking pleater is a wonderful machine to have access to when you want to create fine even pleats.

Once the fabric has been drawn up, the pleats can be pulled out into all kinds of patterns stitched in place and embellished with beads or embroidery to form accent areas. The thread used to draw up the pleats can be left in situ as a special effect. Make a conscious decision as to what colour to use before threading up the machine. The needle artist does not have to work precise stitches over the pleats as with conventional smocking.

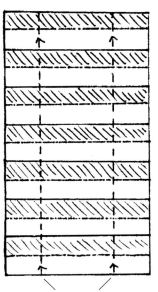 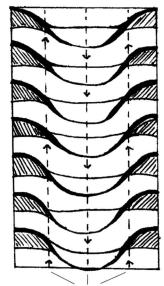 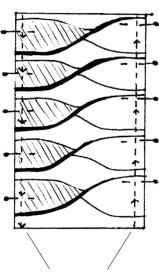

1. Press the tucks in one direction and stitch them down.

2. Stitch up the centre in the opposite direction.

3. Tucks stitched down in the opposite direction on one side.

Sue feels a closeness to the native bushmen people of the Drakensberg where she grew up. They were hunter gatherers surviving extreme weather conditions. Their rock art still adorns many cave walls. The "Flying Geese" arrow heads and leather are all reminiscent of their lifestyles.

Right: ISIBINCA (TO CLOTHE YOUR LOINS) – (Sue Akerman)
The collar on this cape has been created with chamois leather, silk pulled into tiny pleats on a smocking pleater which has then been embellished with fibre urchins/thread and stitching. Cotton classic batting from Fairfield Processing was used in order to allow the cape to hang softly and comfortably.

Detail of textures from – ISIBINCA – and – CHAIN MAIL WAISTCOAT – showing fibre urchins/ layered fabric/tucks/cords.

Photo Copy Transfer

Transferring photos onto fabric can be done in various ways.

Using a photocopy machine, pictures can be transferred directly onto fabric. Fabric transfer mediums are also available. Both these methods give a very clear reproduction of the original; however, if you wish to embroider or embellish the surface is a little stiff. I prefer to transfer photos with a solvent. By applying the solvent and then pressure one can transfer the photocopy onto the fabric.

This method is described below:

TIPS

Remove nail polish before you begin!

Photocopies with large areas of black or grey do not transfer well. When transferring old family photos, choose the ones that have good definition and black and white contrast.

Use a reputable photocopy machine which uses toner not a laser copier.

Use a fine, even weave fabric. This should have a smooth finish. Pre-wash the fabric to make sure the sizing is washed out of it.

Work outdoors or in a well-ventilated area and wash your hands well after using the solvent.

The solvent that I find works best is lacquer thinners (available from paint shops) or pure acetone. (Available from pharmacies)

METHOD

- Make a photocopy of the picture that you intend transferring.
- Cut your fabric larger than the print to be transferred and iron it well.
- Place a piece of cardboard on your work surface and, using masking tape, tape the fabric to it.
- Tape the photocopy, right side down on the fabric. Remember to centre the photocopy. It is not necessary to tape the photocopy on all sides, 2 sides will suffice.
- Lightly wet a piece of muslin with the solvent. Very little solvent is required. You should not be able to squeeze any excess out of the muslin. Dab this onto the back of the photocopy. You do not need to work the whole photocopy at one time. Small areas can be worked at a time.

Photocopy transfers blend well with other fabric images using machine embroidery.

Guinea fowl transferred onto chamois leather.

- With the back of a spoon, rub the area of the photocopy where the solvent has been applied. You will need to apply a LOT of pressure. Take care not to move the photocopy when rubbing. Reapply the solvent if necessary and apply more pressure with the spoon.
- At this stage lift the photocopy and check how much has transferred. Do this with care so that you can replace the print and re-apply the solvent and pressure should the image not have transferred sufficiently well.
- Once the whole image has been transferred, remove the photocopy and air-dry the fabric.
- Heat set with a hot iron working from the back. This transfer should now be permanent and should be washable.

PROBLEM SOLVING

If your image is runny/ unclear/ smudged. Too much solvent was used.

A bad transfer can result from a poor photocopy from a poor machine, not applying enough pressure or solvent, or using the wrong solvent or the wrong fabric.

Ask the photo-copy technician to make the colour as strong as possible.

Do not forget to ask for a mirror image if the design has to face a specific direction, e.g. family portraits etc.

SPECIAL EFFECTS

- Embroider or embellish the photocopies.
- Try transferring onto different types of fabric. Chamois leather takes transfers well.

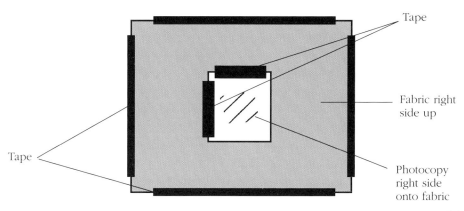

Tape

Fabric right side up

Photocopy right side onto fabric

Tape

DAY COAT –
(Jutta Faulds)

RAY OF HOPE –
(Sue Akerman)

AFRICAN VIBRATIONS –
(Sally Scott)

MOPANI IN THE SPRING –
(Sue Funston)

Chapter II

AFRICAN RHYTHM

CAFÉ AU LAIT –
(Jutta Faulds)
Morning coat

PERUVIAN SYMBOLS –
(Marge Gatter)

Above, left: HEX MAGIC – (Annette McMaster)
Above, right: SUNSPOTS DISRUPT THE RAIN DANCE – (Jutta Faulds)

Bias Windows

These little windows make wonderful highlights or features on a garment. As with a picture frame they draw the eye and make the viewer want to explore them.

METHOD

Cut a square hole in the fabric at the point where you want the window to be. Cut a bias strip of fabric approximately $1^1/_2$" / $3^3/_4$cm wide. With a straight stitch, and right sides together, stitch the binding around the aperture. Now turn the bias strip to the inside of the aperture and the wrong side of the fabric. In other words you are lining the hole. You can leave as little or as much of the lining [bias] as required showing, depending on the effect required. Topstitch the lining in place.

SPECIAL EFFECTS

- Glue a Shisha mirror into the hole.
- Use a contrasting bias to emphasise the hole.
- Use a raw silk or highly contrasting fabric stitched behind the hole.

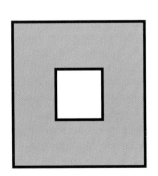

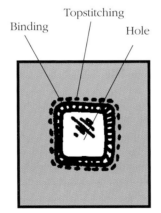

1. Cut a hole in the fabric.

2. Stitch the binding around the hole.

3. Turn the binding to the wrong side and topstitch it in place.

Right: **Detail from** – DAY COAT

Tubes, Fringes and Wrapped Cords

Not everyone likes bits and pieces hanging off their garments, but for those who do, these are a wonderful tactile option. Remember they must be an integral part of the garment and not merely an attachment. They must also be securely fastened. A more interesting result will be obtained by cutting them into different widths and lengths.

Tubes

To make a tube:

Cut the strips 1 inch / 2 ¹/₂cm. wide and as long as you require them to be. (Alter the width as required)

Fold the strip in half lengthways with right sides together.

Stitch along the length of the tube

Turn it inside out.

Neaten off the ends.

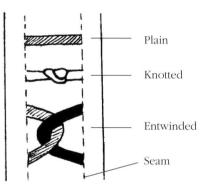

Plain

Knotted

Entwinded

Seam

SPECIAL EFFECTS.

- Use them inserted into seams and interlinking with one another.
- Make wider tubes, iron them flat and then weave them into a bigger piece of fabric.
- Tie knots in them
- Sew beads or buttons onto them.
- Embellish with running stitches, cross-stitch or featherstitch.
- Use paint pens to decorate them.
- Make thicker tubes and stuff with batting. Use these to emphasise a neck edge.
- Sew a small, stuffed fibre urchin onto the end of the tube.

Left: *Detail from* – "EARTH REVISITED" – (Sue Akerman)

Fringes

Tassels and fringes are so very tactile. They remind me of fur or a warm comfy feeling. These can be made in a number of ways and then stitched into a seam as required. This seam should be double stitched to ensure that all the strands are secure.

One can buy wonderful fringes that are available from decorating shops or you can use a combination of wool, thread, cotton, wrapped cords, and bought fringing.

SPECIAL EFFECTS
- Thread some of the fringe with beads, shells, buttons etc.
- Some loosely woven fabrics unravel easily and can make a stunning fringe.

Wrapped Cords

One needs a variety of threads and wools in order to make interesting wrapped cords.

I also add very thin slivers of fabric to my cords on occasion.

Set your machine on the widest Zigzag setting and drop the feeddog.

Lay 2 or 3 threads/wools together and zigzag over them.

Let the stitches work closer together in some areas and further apart in others. This has the effect of the threads being wrapped together.

This cord can be made as long or as short as necessary by continuing to add more cords and threads as you sew.

SPECIAL EFFECTS
- Thread beads onto a long piece of wool or cotton and as you zigzag the cords together, add this beaded cord in. (Be careful not to hit a bead with the machine needle.)
- Feathers can be added into the cord.
- Papermaché tubes can be made, painted and threaded onto your cords or tubes.
- Plait them together to make beautiful braids.

Detail – A RAY OF HOPE – (*See page 26*). *Fabric used for the tubes was cut on the bias.*

Detail – AFRICAN VIBRATIONS – *(See page 26).*
Repetition creates harmony in these squares. The fringe was created with wool and thread and inserted into the seam.

Detail – HOMAGE TO PAUL KLEE – *(See page 40).*
Very effective use of fabric paints on this garment enhance the underlying construction. Note the bias window features. Painted papermaché tubes are an interesting detail on this coat.

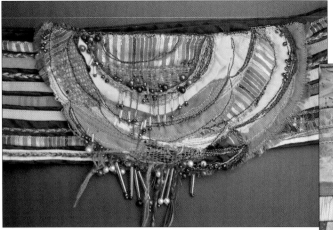

Detail, belt from – A RAY OF HOPE
Beading is a part of the Zulu culture in South Africa in which I was brought up – my love of beads is inherent. Here, bugel beads and a mixture of glass and plastic round beads have been used. The main belt section has had tubes of fabric and braided cords topstitched onto it. Velcro is used to fasten the belt.

Detail of hat – *(See page 40).*
Beautifully hand sewn tubes and berries are the feature on this hat. The top stitching of the tubes is an added feature. The "berries" are made in the same way as fibre urchins are made, except that they are stuffed with batting.

Detail – THE GUARDIAN – *(See page 40/50).*
This thick tube, stuffed with batting and then couched down emphasises the neck opening and makes a very special feature on this garment.

A RAY OF HOPE — (See page 26 front).
(It's hot in Africa you know!) Also made at
a time of political change. I felt a great sense
of optimism for our rebirth as a country.

CAFÉ AU LAIT MORNING COAT —
(See page 27 front).
Simple strip and log cabin piecing form the
base for this coat. Very effective use of prairie
points, buttons and subtle colour changes
make it work so well.

MOPANI IN THE SPRING —
(See page 26 front).
The centre back panel is created with tucks of
fabric – stitched down on either side with
bias strips. This outfit is a tribute to the
intense colours of the Mopani veld in the
Kruger National Park.

AFRICAN VIBRATIONS —
(See page 26 front).
The fringe gives this garment a life of its
own – it says "touch me". The repetition of
the squares within which wonderful colour
changes occur, creates harmony. Note the
hand stitching detail on the lower tassles.
Wonderful sensitivity to the hidden colours in
the African bush, is demonstrated here.
What some people's eyes only read as a drab
brown landscape.

PERUVIAN SYMBOLS –
(Marge Gatter)

WILD KIMONO COAT –
(Sue Akerman)

NIGHT SKY –
(Jutta Faulds)

WAITING FOR WINTER –
(Jutta Faulds)

GOLD DREAM COAT –
(Betty Beekes)

WAITING FOR WINTER –
(Jutta Faulds)

RHYTHMS OF AFRICA —
(Sally Scott)

Chapter III

A CELEBRATION OF LIFE

ZEBRA CROSSING —
(Sally Scott)

ORANGE FIZZ —
(Betty Beekes)

Hand Embroidery

EMBELLISHING WITH HAND EMBROIDERY

The beauty of hand or machine embroidery is that it can be worked at any stage in the construction of a garment. One can start by embellishing pieces of fabric and then stitch other pieces of fabric onto the main embroidered pieces. The pattern piece can then be cut from the larger "created" piece of cloth. Piecing can also be done first using numerous fabrics and then the unit can be embellished with embroidery. Embroidery adds texture, colour and interesting detail to a piece of work. It can also be used to create a focal point.

Thread: When choosing thread for use on clothing do remember that it should be durable and washable. The same applies to Victorian crazy patchwork on clothing. Little "bits and pieces" that are stitched on must be able to stand up to general wear and tear. I don't have any hard and fast rules about thickness or thinness of thread. I use whatever works best to accomplish the effect required for the piece.

Stitches: A word of caution about stitches. Compact or closely worked stitches are best on a garment as they do not run the risk of being caught or pulled.

Fabric: Choose the weight of fabric to suit the choice of stitch, i.e. fabric which will not sag or pull out of shape. It is often a very good rule to work with a piece of muslin at the back of your fabric. You will find that you get a wavy effect or puckering of your fabric if you work too intensely in one area and not enough or not at all in other areas. (Stretching your fabric into hoop, should you encounter this problem.) This will stabilise the fabric and prevent it distorting. This is not to say that you should not have areas of intense embroidery as these can be simply stunning. Try and create areas of intense interest to which the viewer's eye is drawn.

One doesn't need to know a million stitches in order to create a wonderful surface design. A limited range of stitches used is sometimes more successful.

One can group stitches into line, texture and filler stitches.

LINE STITCHES give outline, basic form and rhythm.

These stitches include couching, stem stitch, backstitch, continuous chain and coral stitch.

TEXTURED STITCHES create atmosphere and a tactile surface.

These include French knots, bullion knots, tufting, seed stitches, detached chain and fly stitch.

FILLER STITCHES are used to fill an area, create movement and link shapes together.

SPECIAL EFFECTS
- Try different thickness of thread.
- Vary the tension to create loose and tight stitches.
- Work stitches close together and then far apart.
- Blend different threads together and work the stitch.
- Work stitches in different directions.
- Work stitches in a circle.
- Work the stitches short and then long.
- Do not work the stitches conventionally- e.g. When working a French knot do not pull it tight and thus create a "loopy" French knot.

Note the top stitching of threads and wools to enhance the traditional log cabin patchwork design

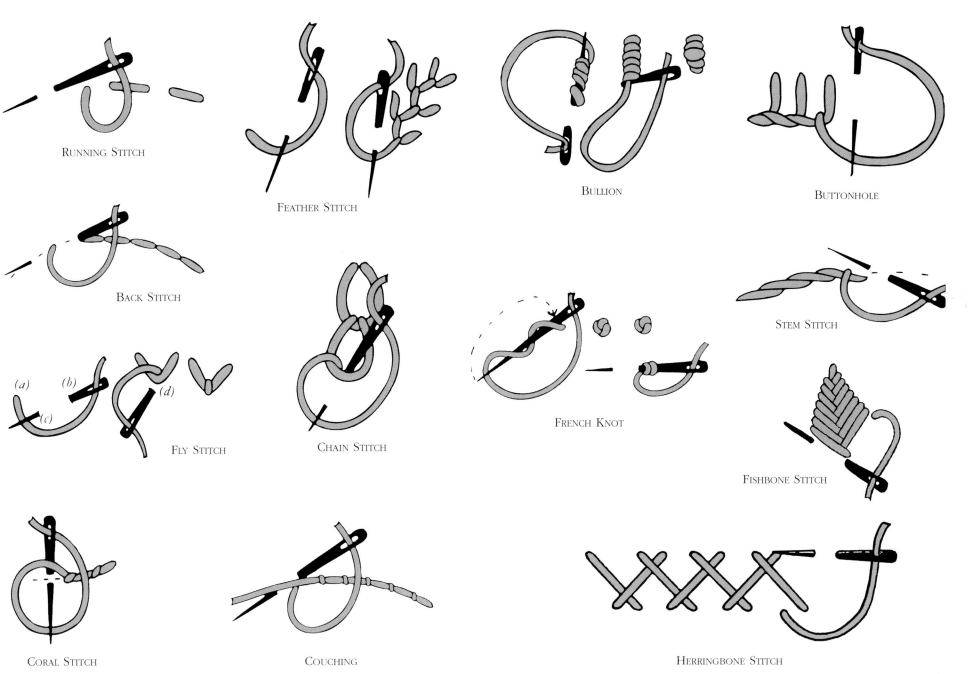

RUNNING STITCH

FEATHER STITCH

BULLION

BUTTONHOLE

BACK STITCH

CHAIN STITCH

FRENCH KNOT

STEM STITCH

(a)   (b)
   (c)   (d)
FLY STITCH

FISHBONE STITCH

CORAL STITCH

COUCHING

HERRINGBONE STITCH

37

ORANGE FIZZ – (Betty Beekes) – *A celebration of kitsch. This was* made with tongue in cheek. It is a wonderful garment with only a few selected stitches used. Mostly feather, buttonhole and running stitches. Plastic barbie shoes/racquets and buttons adorn the coat.

WAITING FOR WINTER – (Jutta Faulds) – *Collars draw one's eye to the neck and shoulders. They need not always be attached, but can be buttoned on. This allows the garment to be versatile.*

KIMONO COAT GONE WILD
An example of how effective ra
The kimono coat is a very comfo
for pattern).

(Akerman) – (See page 34).
...ué and topstitching can be.
...f coat to wear. (See page 72

AFRICAN RHYTHM – *Detail* – *(See page 35 for full outfit).*
The simple stitching between these blocks unifies all these machine
appliquéd pieces.

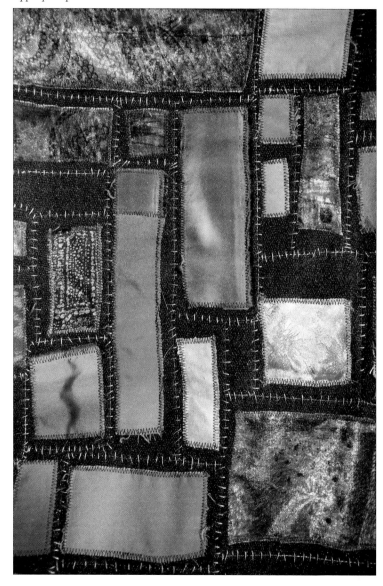

GOLD DREAM COAT – (Betty Beekes) – *(See page 34 for whole coat).*
A black fabric with some printing inspired this piece. Note the different
thicknesses of thread used and the combination of stitches and beads.

SUNSPOTS DISRUPT
THE RAINDANCE —
(Jutta Faulds)

PRAIRIE POINT MAGIC —
(Nina Lawrence)

THE GUARDIAN — (Jutta Faulds)

HOMAGE TO PAUL KLEE —
(Jutta Faulds)

A HAT FOR ALL SEASONS —
(Nina Lawrence)

Chapter IV

EXOTIC FANTASIES

FREEDOM FLIGHT – (Sue Akerman) –
(See page 7 for the front view).

DREAM CATCHING AGAIN –   (Sue Akerman)

ISIBINCA –   (Sue Akerman)

Appliqué

There are many ways in which to apply one fabric to another or for that matter thread to fabric:

HAND APPLIQUÉ – The traditional way of hand turning under the raw edges of a motive and stitching it in place on the base layer of fabric.

MACHINE APPLIQUÉ – The use of a very close machine satin stitch around the edges of a motive. This technique gives a very naive look with the shapes having a very definite outline.

MACHINE APPLIQUÉ with a difference. The traditional hand and machine appliqué techniques are widely written about.

This is the method that I will be discussing.

CREATIVE MACHINE APPLIQUÉ (with a difference)

This technique is actually more like a machine embroidery type appliqué. At the same time as applying the pieces of fabric you will be creating different effects with the stitching threads. With this method you work layers of stitching over each other in order to firmly apply the fabric or thread to the base layer of fabric. I generally use a straight stitch on the machine and drop the feed dog so as to have total control of the fabric.

MATERIALS REQUIRED

A base layer of fabric, a piece of double-sided vilene, all the bits of fabric to be applied and lots of different coloured machine cottons.

METHOD

Iron doublesided vilene onto the backs of all the appliqué pieces.

Onto a base layer of fabric, place all the bits of fabric that are to be applied and with a hot iron secure them in position. All the fabric should stick to the base layer.

With a running stitch, work around all the motifs. You may wish to work around the motifs with quite a few rows of stitching in order to secure them firmly. Pieces can also be secured in place with a zigzag, rather than a straight stitch. By couching thicker threads over the edges of the motives certain parts of the appliqué can be enhanced.

Detail from –
DREAM CATCHING AGAIN –

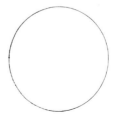

1. Cut motif out of fabric.

2. Turn under a small seam and baste.

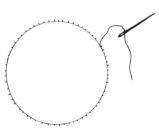

3. With tiny slip stitches attach the motif to the base fabric.

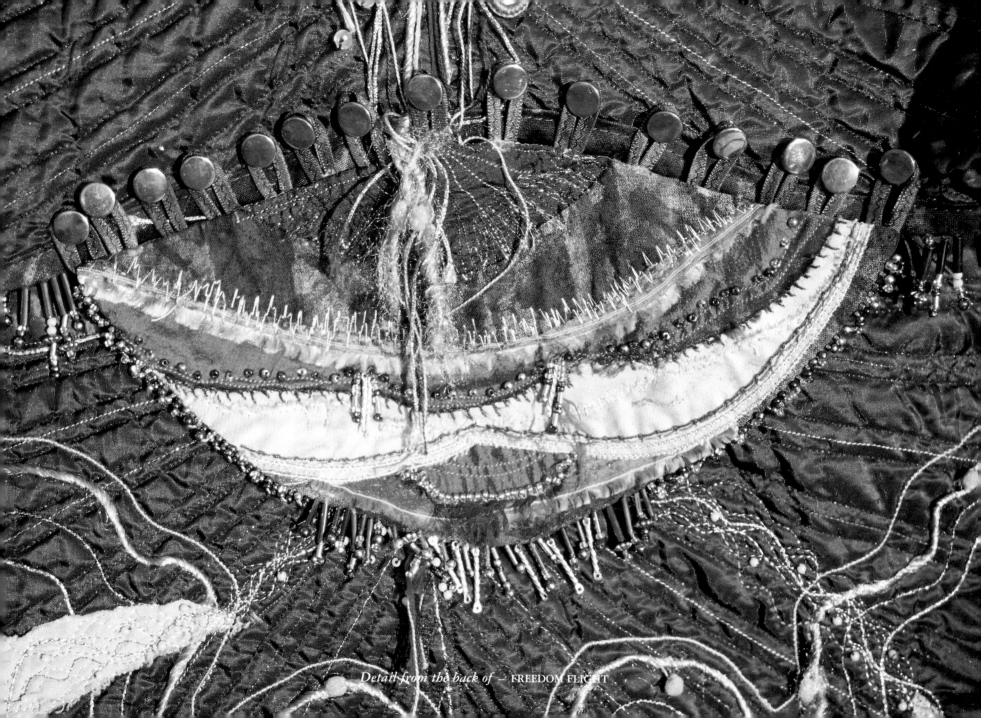

Detail from the back of — FREEDOM FLIGHT

Prairie Points

Prairie points are an old favourite, and their varied use will never die. They look wonderful repeated and sewn into seams or used individually in varying sizes.

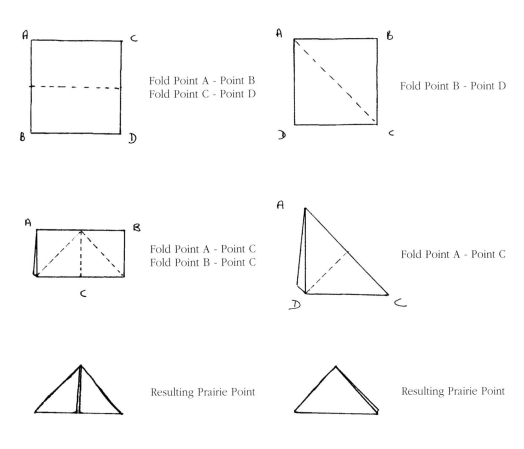

Fold Point A - Point B
Fold Point C - Point D

Fold Point B - Point D

Fold Point A - Point C
Fold Point B - Point C

Fold Point A - Point C

Resulting Prairie Point

Resulting Prairie Point

INDIVIDUAL POINTS

Cut squares of varying sizes. Fold in half to form a triangle and then in half again.

Or fold in half to form a rectangle and then fold the outer corners on the fold to the centre to create a triangle.

Back detail from – CAFÉ AU LAIT – MORNING COAT
(See page 27 front view).

Continuous Points

1. Cut a strip of fabric 4 ½ inches wide (12cm), and as long as required for the amount of prairie points needed.
2. Draw a line along the entire length of the fabric 4 inches (10cm) in from the edge.
3. Now draw lines at 4 inch (10cm) intervals at right angles to the line already drawn.
4. Cut the fabric on these marked short lines up to the point where they meet the long line.
5. Fold the squares in one direction in order to create a triangle.
6. Fold them a second time in the opposite direction.

Stitch the length of prairie points into a seam.

Trim off excess fabric.

N.B. Do not use thick fabric for prairie points as they can make a seam too bulky once they have been stitched into it.

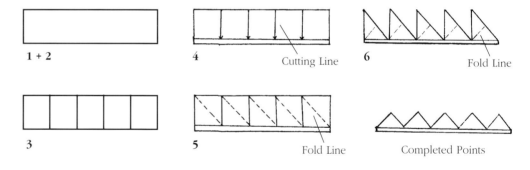

SPECIAL EFFECTS (with prairie points)

- Decorate with buttons and paint.
- Slot one into the other.
- Use different sizes rather than a uniform size.
- Small accents of intense colour create a dramatic effect.
- Group them rather than having them on their own scattered around. In Africa we say, "A herd of buffalo looks better than one lone bull!" A group of anything has more impact than one lone soldier. A word of caution however, more is not always better!

Detail – PRAIRIE POINT MAGIC
Note the amazing use of superimposed prairie points.

Fabric Painting

It takes a brave heart to pick up a can of paint and embellish an already completed piece of work, not quite knowing how it is going to affect the piece. On the other had it is an incredibly liberating feeling once complete.

Adding a touch of paint to a problem area can be a quick fix solution to a problem, where embroidery might have taken hours.

Paints come in various forms. Spray paints in cans, fabric pen markers, liquid paints that need to be applied with a brush. As long as they are fabric friendly and permanent I use what is available. Experimentation is the key to success with both dyeing and painting of fabrics.

Paints can obviously be applied in more than one way. For a start the fabric can either be dry or wet. The paints can be used diluted for a runny or gentle effect. By painting with a brush one can produce more definite marks, and a smudged effect can be attained with fingers or a sponge. In order to remove colour and create a speckled effect paint the fabric and lay it out in the sun and then sprinkle course salt onto areas of the surface.

The salt will absorb colour and leave a mottled effect. Another way of removing colour is to sprinkle bleach onto the fabric.

Then there are all the colour permutations of adding black and white to clear colours and mixing colours.

BLOCK PRINTS

Printing with blocks is an age-old technique, used in pattern making. Patterns surround us in our lives. Think about using corks or the ends of pencils or dowel sticks, and fingers just to mention a few. Should you make your own block then foam is a good medium.

Using a firm, dense piece of foam either cut or burn out a shape. Place paint onto a flat surface and dab the sponge into it. The paint should be of a fairly thick consistency. Always have a practise run on a spare piece of fabric. Apply pressure evenly when printing onto the fabric. If you wish to apply more than one colour at the same time, brush the colour onto the print block and then print.

Gaudy plastic flowers and fabric paints adorn this piece — made by Jutta Faulds. The beauty of fabric paint being that it can be done at a last minute to add more colour or detail.

Dyeing Fabric

Dyeing fabric is a wonderful option and can generate amazing effects. There is always an element of uncertainty with dyeing as to what the end result will be. This makes the process exciting. Experimentation makes one more confident with this technique. Many books have been written on the subject and should you wish to pursue this technique I would suggest that you acquire one of them. At this point in my career I tend to stick to painting as I feel as if I want more control over the end result of the piece of work.

BLEACH

Bleach can remove colour in the most unpredictable way and create wonderful patterns. Bleach is toxic and should be used with care. Some people prefer not to use bleach on fabric, as they fear the long-term effects on the fabric. It can be applied with a brush, a squirt bottle with a nozzle or a spray bottle. Once the bleach has created the required effect I wash the fabric in a little vinegar and water.

RESISTS

Resists are used when specific areas of fabric need to be shielded from paint. The resist will stop the paint from running into areas that you do not want to be painted. It is applied when the fabric is dry. I make a solution of water and corn flour. Resists can be applied through a bottle with a nozzle. The fabric needs to be sun dried once the resist has been applied. The resist is washed out once the fabric is painted and the paint is dry.

Left: THE GUARDIAN – *The inclusion of these natural 'found pieces' make a statement by the artist, about the message she needs to convey. This is a dual purpose garment. It looks beautiful hanging on a wall as well as on the human form.*

Fibre Urchins — Yo-Yo's

I have chosen to call these fibre urchins as they remind me of the sea urchins of pumpkin shells which are found in abundance along the South African coast.

1. Make a template of a circle out of cardboard or plastic. Remember that your completed urchin will be substantially smaller because of the gathering process. It will be reduced to just over half the original size.
2. Trace around the circle onto the fabric and cut it out.
3. Thread a needle with cotton.
4. Turn under a 3 mm or ¼ inch seam allowance, and work a running stitch around the edge of the circle.
5. Draw or gather the running stitch up so that the raw edge is on the inside. Work a double stitch to end off.
6. Stitch the urchin onto the garment using a buttonhole stitch.

SPECIAL EFFECTS

- Before gathering up the urchin glue a Shisha mirror into the centre. Allow the shisha mirror to be visible when complete. This will mean that you do not pull the gathers in as tightly as normal.
- Let tassels hang freely from the centre.
- Place a piece of contrast or shiny fabric into the centre of the urchin and puff it out through the centre.
- Fill the centre with beads or buttons.
- Don't turn the 3mm raw edge to the inside, but leave it showing on the outside. This creates a frayed ruffle around the neck of the urchin.

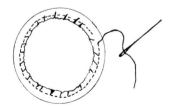
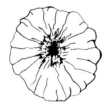

Fibre Urchin Completed

Fibre Urchin with Shisha Mirror in the Centre

Right: ISIBINCA — *Fibre urchins of all shapes, sizes and treated in different ways, offset this collar of rouched silk and chamois leather. (See full garment on page 50).*

Detail – A HAT FOR ALL SEASONS – (Nina Lawrence)
*Prairie points and this beautiful edging on this wrap, together with the dyed lining make an
incredibly rich statement. Take note of the belt with all the tubes and the inclusion of knitted fabric
on the bodice. The fabric (hand dyed) was torn into strips before being knitted.*

Left:
ISIBINCA —
(Sue Akerman)

Right:
THE GUARDIAN —
(Jutta Faulds)

A COAT FOR AN
AFRICAN GARDENER —
(Jutta Faulds)

Above: **Detail from** – SUNBIRD – (Jutta Faulds) – *(See page 55).*
As an artist Jutta's concerns are for the environment, creating awareness of its fragility for the wearer, her body pieces provide a shelter, a protection against outside intrusive elements, a shield behind which to find peace. For the onlooker they are beacons in an evermore joyless world.

AFRICAN PRAYER RUG – (Jutta Faulds)
(See page 55).
These garments are made to be worn by people but also look wonderful hanging, making an artistic statement on a wall. The challenge is twofold – Jutta challenges the outsider as to "what is wearable" – and she challenges herself to make these garments work both 3 dimensionally as well as on a "flat" surface.

Chapter V

IF YOU DON'T WEAR IT HANG IT

$\mathcal{S}$ee these garments hanging on the following page.

Bag from – A COAT FOR AN AFRICAN GARDENER *– (See page 54).*

A COAT FOR AN AFRICAN GARDENER — (Jutta Faulds)

CROSSES FOR AFRICA — (Jutta Faulds)

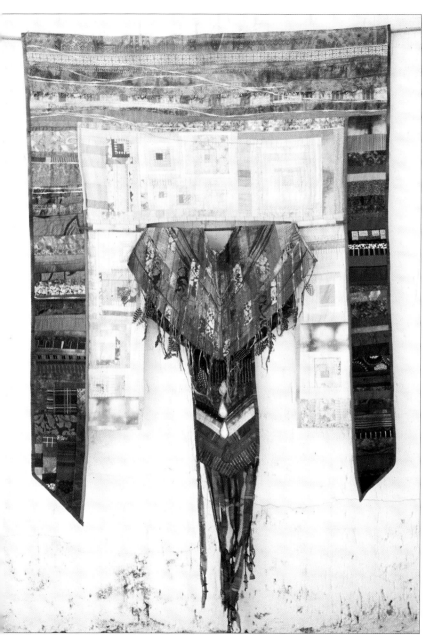

AN AFRICAN PRAYER RUG — (Jutta Faulds)

SUNBIRD — (Jutta Faulds)

Machine Embroidery

All of us work with different machines and through practice you will be able to master this technique and further enhance the surface appeal of the fabric.

Machine embroidery is wonderfully exciting and relatively quick in comparison with hand embroidery.

It can be compared with an artist painting with a palette of paint colours, only that here the machine is the brush and the cottons the paint.

Important points to remember

- Use a darning foot on the machine.
- Drop the feed dog on the machine.
- Loosen the top tension. The bottom tension can also be loosened for different effects.
- Set stitch length on 0.
- Place the fabric into a spring embroidery hoop to keep it firm. This will prevent puckering. The hoop can easily be moved around while stitching.
- Relax. You are in total control of the fabric.
- Before stitching bring the bobbin thread up to the top surface and work 3 or 4 stitches in one place in order to anchor the threads. Use this technique to end the line of stitching.
- Apply a steady pressure to the foot pedal. I find that a faster speed is often easier than working too slowly.
- Your hands will need to move the fabric at a steady speed.
- Buy a bobbin case that is only used for embroidery as one often needs to loosen the tension on the bobbin case. In this way you will not be tampering with the normal machine tension. You can use this bobbin case for all thicker threads that need to be wound onto a bobbin and are worked from the bottom. Some machine companies market a specific bobbin case for machine embroidery.
- Special machine embroidery needles are available. You may need to purchase heavy-duty needles for heavier fabrics and leather.
- Change needles regularly as they become blunt. Discard needles after each project

Many of the machines have their own set of embroidery stitches. These can create wonderful effects when used as topstitching in areas, however they can become monotonous if overused.

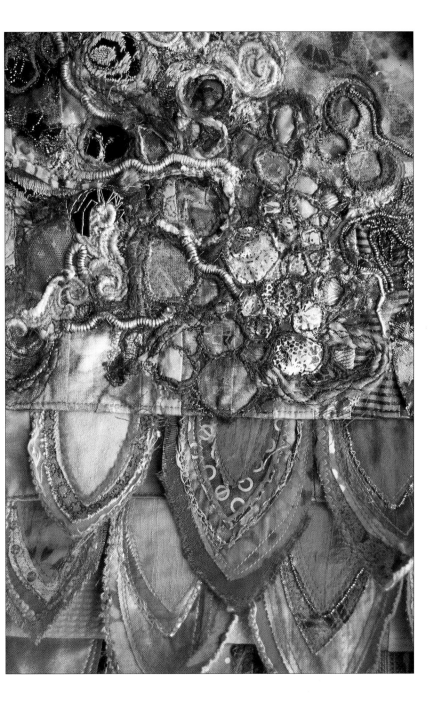

I rely mostly on running or straight stitch for effect and for topstitching. A Zigzag stitch is useful for couching threads onto fabric as well as for effect.

The machine buttonhole stitch is an exciting stitch to use when couching.

Couching and topstitching can be used to enhance very traditional piecing.

With this method of free stitching one can apply pieces of fabric, thick and thin yarns and threads as well as cords. I have used a rather novel idea with silkworm cocoons. Cut them in half, discard the chrysalis and then stitch them onto the fabric in a floral shape. They become wonderful sunflowers.

SPECIAL EFFECTS

There are a million, here are but a few.

- Use spray paint to enhance your embroidery once complete.
- Use a combination of thick and thin thread. They will enhance each other and create depth.
- Do not work the whole surface with the same intensity.
- Small pieces of net in areas can create very subtle colour and textural changes.
- Do not be afraid to cut holes in your embroidery and then stitch across these holes creating a cobweb effect.
- Add hand stitching, beads and sequins.
- Embellish the machine embroidery with fabric paint.

Experiment with your machine tension, both top and bottom. You will find all kinds of exciting things happening. By loosening the bottom tension (bobbin) and tightening the top tension, more of the bobbin thread will be pulled to the top surface.

Opposite page: Detail – CROSSES FOR AFRICA
Note how the topstitching is used to enhance the image of the cross and is then repeated.

Left: Detail – SUNBIRD
This colourful rich surface is created with layers of stitching, topstitching and painting.

Free Standing Motifs

All 3 dimensional "extras" that are added to a garment must be securely attached. Bear in mind that it is going to be worn and laundered. Secure all the edges well so that they do not unravel.

There are numerous ways of doing this.

1. **USE OF THE ZIG-ZAG STITCH**

   Zigzag around the edges.

2. **STITCHWITCHERY**

   In order to stabilise or make the fabric firmer, use a layer of double-sided adhesive (double sided vilene) between 2 layers of fabric. Using a hot iron fuse the 2 layers of fabric with the vilene. These edges are fairly stable, but a zigzag can be worked around the edge. Heavier thread can be used to couch around the edges. Cut out the shapes.

3. **USE OF NET**

   Any weight of fabric, including net can be used in a double layer to create a free-standing motif. Fuse these layers using double-sided vilene. Always fuse the fabric, then stitch around the shape and work any embroidery required onto it. Cut out the shape with a sharp pair of scissors. Use the embroidery scissors with a curved cutting edge.

4. **USE OF WIRE**

   Edges can also be wired in order to give more form and flexibility. Run a fine wire along the edge of the motive and work a zigzag stitch over the top of it.

5. **USE OF ORGANZA**

   Always secure organza and fine fabrics into a hoop when working with them. Only cut them out once the motif is completely stitched.

6. **HEMMED EDGES**

   When needing a well-finished edge, cut out 2 identical shapes and with right sides together, stitch around the edge of the shape, being sure to leave a hole through which it can be turned.

   Clip the edges, and turn inside out.
   Slip stitch the hole closed, iron and secure in place.
   These kinds of motifs can also be stuffed with batting to give a padded effect.

7. **BITS AND PIECES**

   Bits and pieces of fabric or thread caught between net. Lay down a piece of net and sprinkle bits of fabric and thread onto them. Place another piece of net over this. Stitch around the edge of the motif with a zigzag or a straight stitch and then cut out. Work some embroidery or stitching over the surface of the net in order to secure the pieces.

8. **BURNING THE EDGES**

   For a more organic look or when the effect required is not that of a formally finished edge, this technique becomes an option. I would suggest that if the garment is to be worn regularly that more conventional ways of finishing edges are used. This is a wonderful option for wall quilts.

   When burning fabric I use a candle and always work with a wet towel under the area that is being burnt. Work small areas at one time. Burn a small area and then extinguish the flame with another wet towel before moving on to the next area. Some fabrics burn faster than others and so you should always be at the ready to extinguish the flames. Accidents happen awfully quickly. It would probably be better to work outdoors.

These tubes and square parcels are hanging details from Nina Lawrence's belt. Note what a special feature the top stitching and buttons make.

These leaves were made from hand painted silk – two leaf shapes were cut, stitched together, turned inside out and top stitched. The leaves of page 64 were made by snipping silk into tiny pieces – laying it between two layers of net and top stitching these snippets in place.

Detail from a garment – (Marge Gatter). Various thicknesses of fabric were used in the creation of these 3D flowers and leaves – chiffon voil with wire satin stitched onto the edge, allow the petals to stand free. The centres have been made by working machine embroidery onto fusible web.

AN AFRICAN PRAYER RUG –
(Jutta Faulds)
*This low cut neck piece accentuates
the beautiful line of the shoulders
and back. (Also page 53/55).*

A COAT FOR AN AFRICAN GARDENER – (Jutta Faulds)
(Also page 52/54).

Chapter VI

IF YOU DON'T WEAR IT
CUT IT UP
AND REARRANGE IT

Cushions for All Seasons

Once a garment is complete – scraps are kept in a plastic see through packet. This makes life very easy when piecing a quick cushion – a small amount of hand or machine embroidery and Voila!

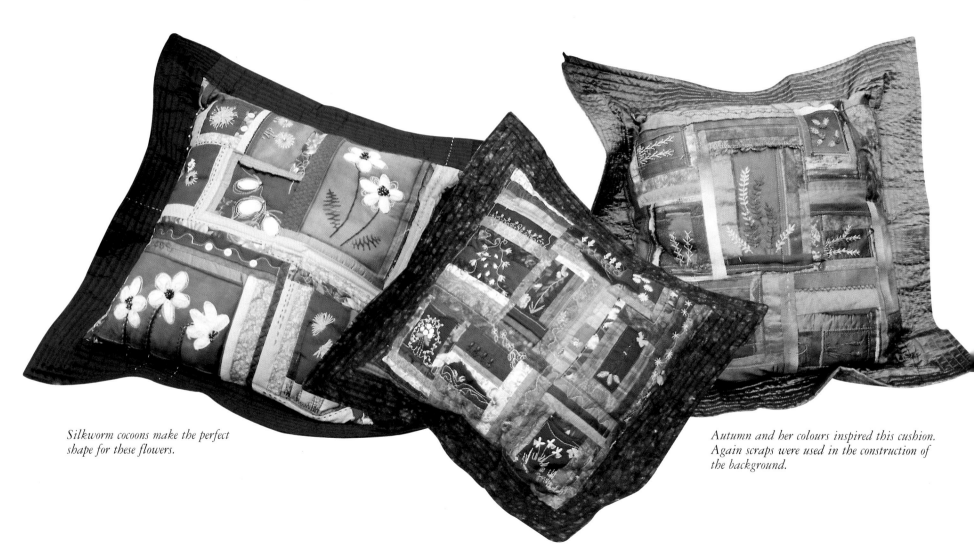

Silkworm cocoons make the perfect shape for these flowers.

Autumn and her colours inspired this cushion. Again scraps were used in the construction of the background.

Double sided vilene was laid onto the base fabric, and all the bits of fabric, net, lace and wool were placed onto this. It was well ironed and then machine embroidered. A few hand stitches completed the exercise.

Crinkled fabric that has been stitched into 3 dimensional leaves, beading and thread embellishments make this a very tactile piece of work.

Designing Basic Belts

A belt should be firm enough to maintain its shape, but flexible enough to feel comfortable and mould to the body's shape. To stiffen the belt, use either vilene or quilting with dense batting inserted as the middle layer.

Belts can be fastened with fabric ties, velcro or buckles and buttons.

Fabrics should be firm enough to hold their shape. When working out the size of the belt, the waist measurement must be taken and the size then calculated. Always have a practice run with an inexpensive fabric to make sure that the size and fit is correct. To make a thin wrap around belt; double the waist measurement and add as much as is needed for the ties.

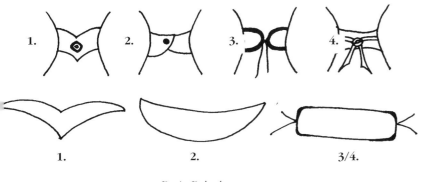

Basic Belt shapes

Attaching Buttons

To prevent buttons from tearing very fine fabric, place a small piece of fabric (of a thinner nature) at the back of the fine fabric and then stitch the button in position. See diagram below.

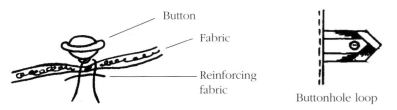

Button

Fabric

Reinforcing fabric

Buttonhole loop

Chapter VII

DRESSING IT UP – PATTERNS
COLLARS – BELTS – BUTTONS

Collars

When a layman thinks of a collar his thoughts go automatically to traditional shirt and jacket collars. Collars can, however be the most beautiful addition to a garment, and can be made to all shapes and sizes. They tend to emphasise the shoulder and neck area and have been worn since the earliest historic times.

Collars can be permanently attached with stitching and are therefore an integral part in the construction of a garment, or they can be added on by being buttoned in position. When buttoned on, the traditional use of buttonholdes and buttons can be utilised. Buttonhole loops made from tubes of fabric also make a very nice feature when stitched into a seam. Tubes must be ironed flat and folded as shown in the diagram.

IDEAS FOR DIFFERENT COLLARS

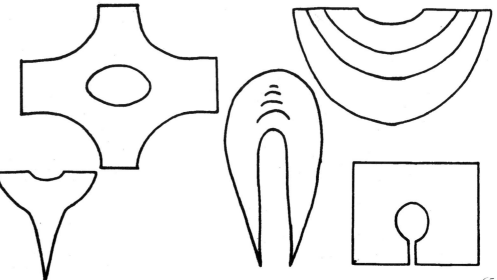

Potential Pattern

I'm sure that by the time you come to read this book you have either mastered the use of commercial patterns or have created your own set of basic patterns. Commercial patterns can be easily simplified and adjusted. Once you have altered a pattern, it is always a good idea to cut a mock garment out of cheap fabric, stitch it together and make sure that it fits well. When heavily embellishing fabrics the more simple the pattern the better. The use of simple patterns will also facilitate good design development. Try avoiding darts when making these garments as they create bulk.

Every human is a different size and shape. There are no end of combinations in height, width and weight. The right proportion of line, form, colour and texture are essential in order to create an aesthetically pleasing garment.

The Japanese Kimono shape is a very pleasing and easy shape to work with. This coat is also very snug to wear. The square sleeve of the Kimono can be altered to a tapered sleeve. This pattern is really worth trying.

THE EFFECT OF LINE ON A GARMENT

Lines can be created by colour placement, fabric selection and embellishment.

Horizontal lines widen the figure and shorten height. These lines are suitable for the slim, tall individuals.

Diagonal lines flatter almost any figure. These are slimming lines.

Circular lines place emphasis on certain parts of the body. Use them to emphasise the upper body and face.

Vertical lines are slimming.

Straight lines are strong.

Curved lines are soft and graceful.

KEEP THE PATTERN STRAIGHT AND SIMPLE.

Remember these words, as they will make your life a whole lot easier.

I am including a pattern of a basic waistcoat, tapered sleeve Kimono coat, and a cape. Lengthen the waistcoat for a gillet pattern. These patterns will have to be enlarged according to instructions and scale. By studying these patterns you will see just how simple they need to be.

Use the patterns as a guide and then alter them to suit your needs. Enlarge the armholes, lengthen them, shorten them, add on collars – there are a multitude of options.

Side Seams (Lateral Thinking)

Try not be bogged down with conventional garment sewing techniques. Side seams need not be joined in the conventional way, but can very easily and effectively be joined with ties or tubes. Try joining them with another strip of fabric that buttons to both front and back. This makes the construction of the garment both simple and unique. See diagram below.

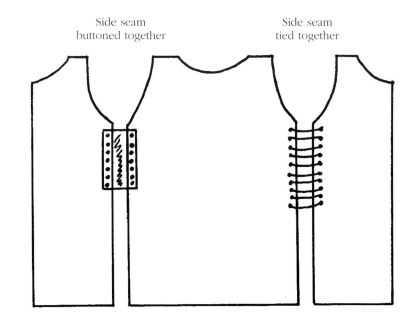

Side seam buttoned together   Side seam tied together

VARIATIONS ON WAISTCOAT SHAPES

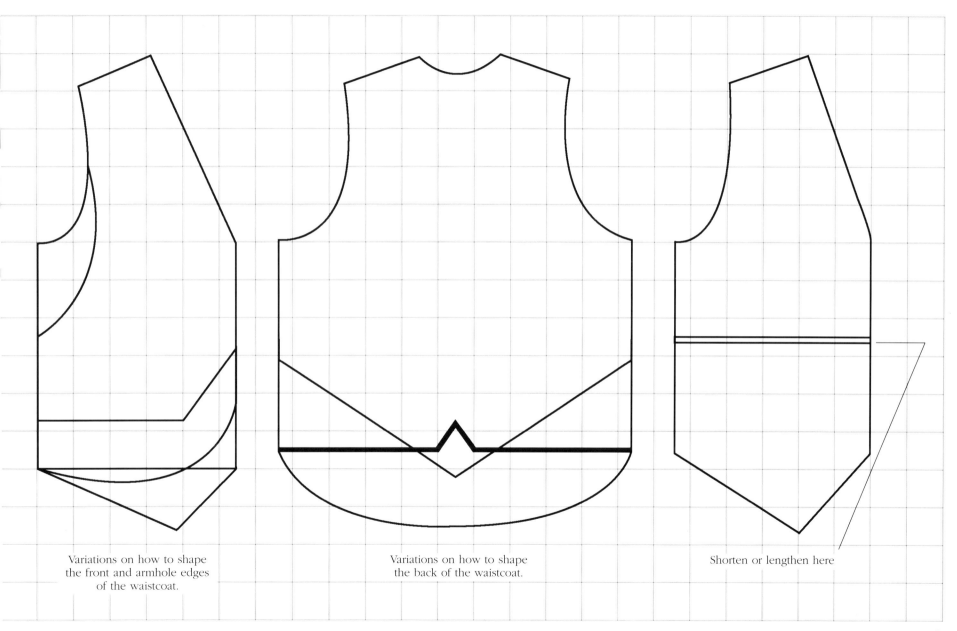

Variations on how to shape the front and armhole edges of the waistcoat.

Variations on how to shape the back of the waistcoat.

Shorten or lengthen here

WAISTCOAT FRONT

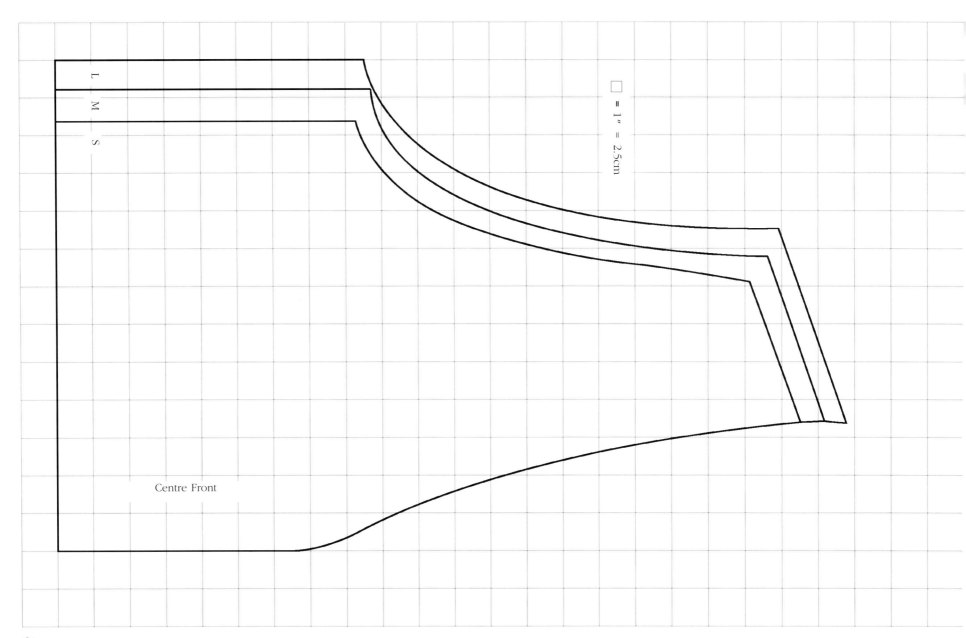

L

M

S

☐ = 1" = 2.5cm

Centre Front

WAISTCOAT BACK

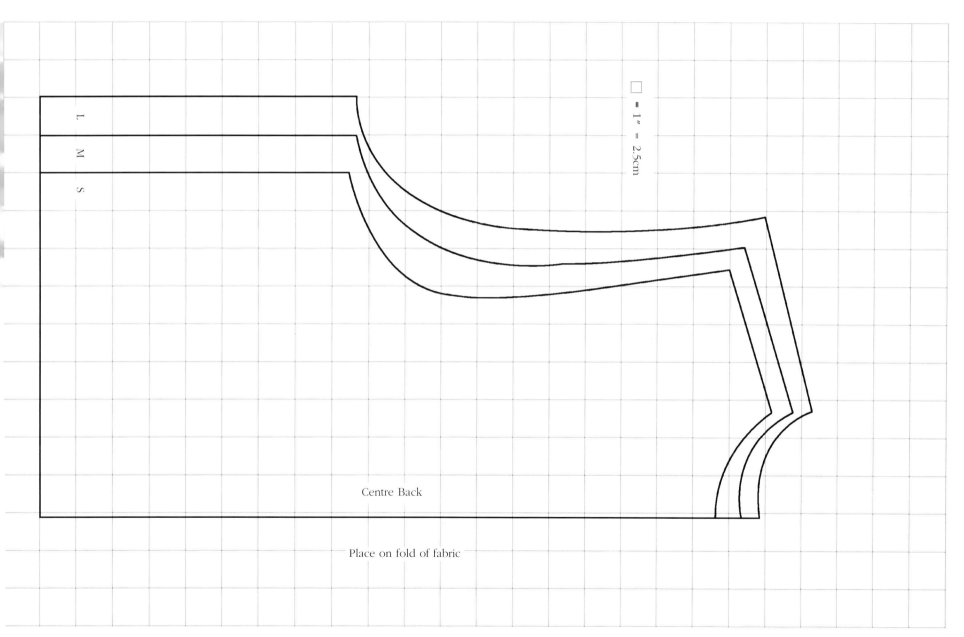

L

M

S

☐ = 1" = 2.5cm

Centre Back

Place on fold of fabric

Discovering Design

Definition: A drawing, plan or sketch made to serve as a pattern from which to work. The arrangement of detail.

When designing a garment consider the whole piece rather than designing individual sections of the garment, so that the garment works as a whole. Pattern pieces are often cut individually and the shape of the body needs to be taken into account. This makes the design process more difficult than a work that will hang flat. The back of a garment is no less important just because it cannot be seen by the wearer. In fact it is often the back of a garment that has the greatest impact.

Repetition works well in design. It often gives structure to a piece of work.

All designs need to have areas of heightened interest as well as quieter areas. The area of heightened interest or the focal point should not be so strong that the eye is held in that place, and does not travel to any other parts of the garment. It should also not be so weak that it does not catch the eye. When making clothing be very careful about the placement of the focal point. It can accent areas of the body that in fact you were trying to hide!

Good design usually emanates from a certain amount of good planning and the rest left to trial and error and instinct.

When we design we are seeking a perfect balance. We are shifting weights, colours, values, lines and forms in order to centre or balance the work.

By experimenting with design problems you will learn how best to solve them. Feel free to explore new methods, as there are no fixed rules.

Exercise: Try using cut-outs like the ones opposite as a window and slide them over newspaper cuttings or pictures in magazines. This will give you plenty of design options. You will instinctively know what looks right. This technique can also be used for guidance with colour choice and distribution.

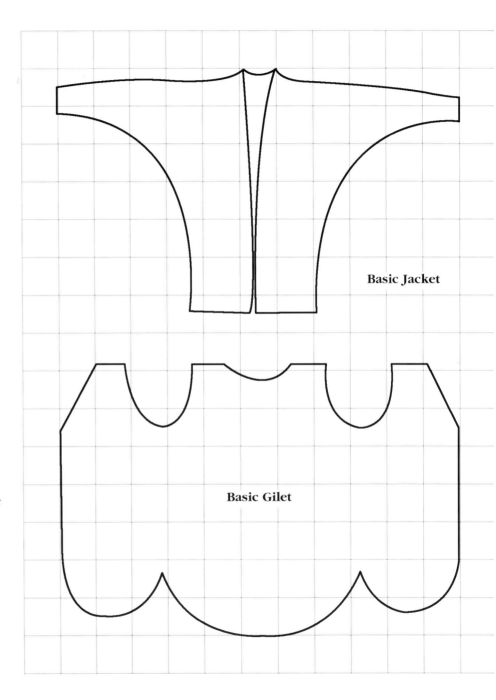

Basic Jacket

Basic Gilet

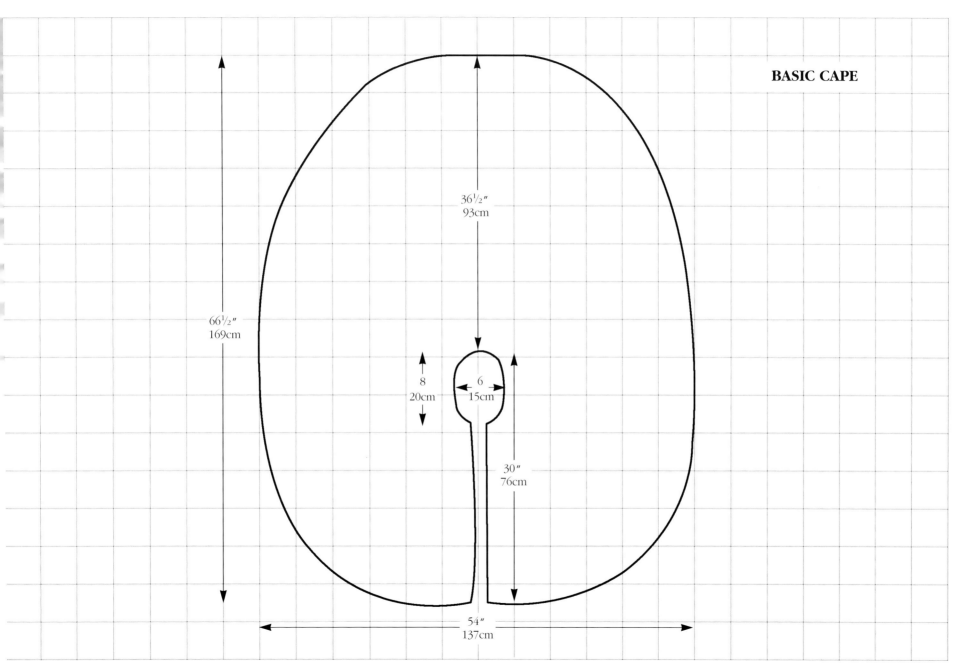

BASIC CAPE

$36\frac{1}{2}''$
93cm

$66\frac{1}{2}''$
169cm

8
20cm

6
15cm

30"
76cm

54"
137cm

Kimono Coat

- Cut the pattern pieces out of newsprint or brown paper.
- Cut the pattern out of fabric: 1 main body piece
                                        1 neck band
                                        2 sleeves
- With right sides together stitch the sleeves to the main body piece, matching them at the shoulder and centre sleeve markings.

FOR A QUILTED COAT

1. Cut batting and identical linings and repeat as above.
2. Quilt the coat, with the batting between the front and the back.
3. Stitch the side and underarm seams.
4. Bind these side seams and the sleeve openings.
5. Stitch the front band on, remembering to clip the square corners at the neck edge (diagram 5)
6. Insert batting into the front band, and turn it to the inside and slipstitch in place.
7. Quilt the front band.
8. Wear it!

FOR AN UNQUILTED LOOK

1. Cut a lining to match the main body and the sleeves. Stitch the lining of the main body piece and sleeves together.
2. With right sides together, pin the lining to the outer fabric.
3. Stitch around the sleeve openings. Stitch the underarm and side seams together as well as the bottom of the 2 fronts [leave the 2 fronts and neck edge open].
4. Turn the garment the correct way around.
5. Press.
6. Attach the band to the front sections and neck area.
7. Turn the band in half and press.
8. Topstitch it in place.
9. Add more topstitching so as to give the band more body.
10. Wear it!

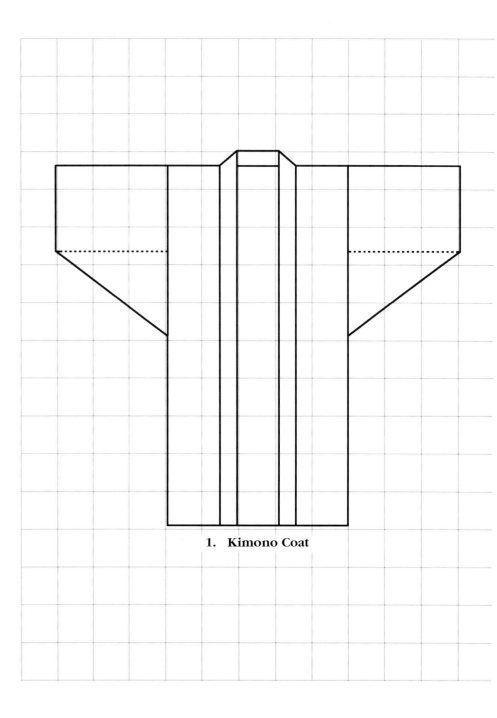

1. Kimono Coat

KIMONO COAT WITH DIAGONALLY CUT SLEEVE

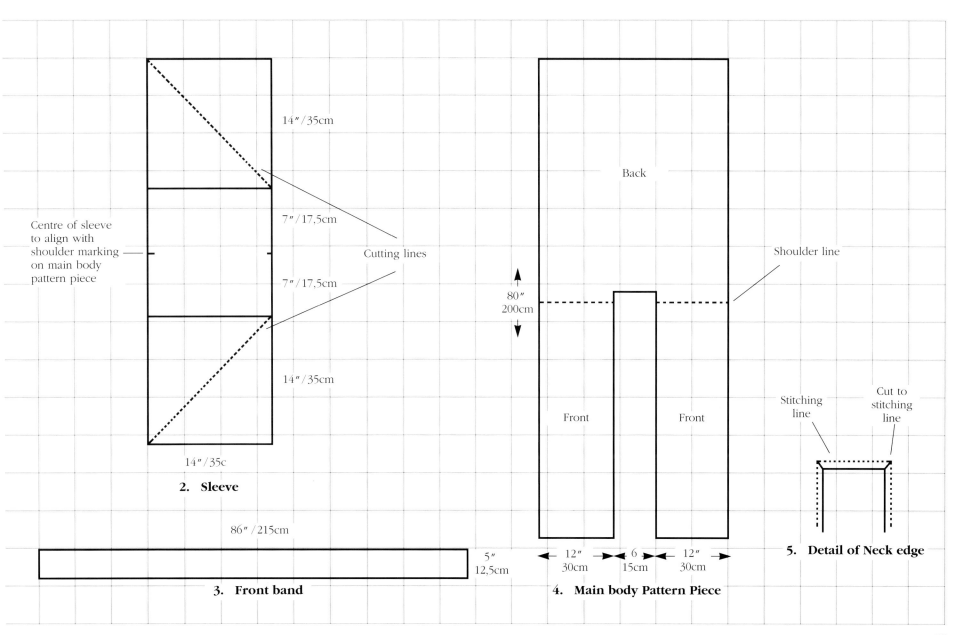

14″/35cm

7″/17,5cm

Centre of sleeve
to align with
shoulder marking
on main body
pattern piece

Cutting lines

7″/17,5cm

14″/35cm

14″/35c

2. Sleeve

Back

Shoulder line

80″
200cm

Front

Front

86″/215cm

5″
12,5cm

3. Front band

12″
30cm

6
15cm

12″
30cm

4. Main body Pattern Piece

Stitching
line

Cut to
stitching
line

5. Detail of Neck edge

Piecing and Patching

Piecing or patching is simply the name given to the technique of sewing different pieces of fabric together. These may have been precisely cut or randomly torn.

When creating a garment one has a few options to choose from when making the fabric.

1. You can choose to work with an entire piece of cloth and then embellish with embroidery, appliqué or quilting.
2. You can piece together an entire surface and then cut your pattern out of this pieced fabric. This too can be embellished with paint, embroidery or quilting.
3. Another method of working is to cut the pattern out of a base cloth material like muslin. Lay this out flat. Then sew the pieces of fabric together, carefully placing them where needed on top of the muslin. These can then be attached to the muslin. The muslin is used as a guide as to how big or small the patches should be.

One can get bogged down with traditional strip or string piecing and then of course, log cabin. All of these techniques can be very exciting if applied in different ways, rather than adhering to old traditions. Always challenge the systems that you know and believe that there are different ways of doing things. You will be surprised at the innovative ways that you find to achieve your objective.

Traditional patterns on clothing may need to be scaled down. These patterns are often too large on garments.

Strip and Seminole patchwork can be used effectively in garments when strips of various widths are sewn together and then cut and resewn to create patterns.

Repetition of colour, pattern and design creates harmony and stability.

LOG CABIN PIECING

Options to vary the log cabin design are endless. Here are a few.

1. Start with an irregular square shape in the centre and stitch the strips around that in a random order.

2. Start the centre of the log cabin with a Shisha mirror block or a bias window.
3. Stitch piping around the centre square and then continue with strip piecing. This will emphasize the centre.
4. A triangle works well as a starting point. Build one side bigger than the other.
5. Use different size strips.

WHOLE CLOTH

A single piece of fabric can be rather monotonous. It can be slashed at any point and feathers, fringes, tubes etc. can be inserted into the seam to create interest.

Striped fabric can be cut up, the stripes realigned and then re-stitched together so as to break the monotony of the stripes.

A STARTING POINT – How to begin

Once the dreaming is done and the creative juices are flowing, draw a rough sketch of what you are going to do.

Decide on colour combinations.

Cut a pattern out of muslin and lay it out. I do this for a number of reasons.

1. It gives me a starting point.
2. It gives me direction as to how big I have to work.
3. Creates a stable surface for me to work on.
4. Allows me to fold it all up and put it away for a while and then work on the piece at a later stage without disturbing it.
5. Now begin the piecing.

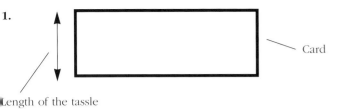

1.

Card

Length of the tassle

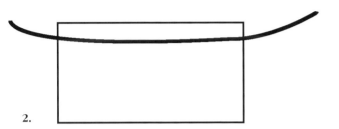

2.

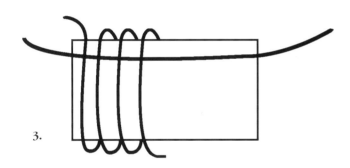

3.

Thick Tassels

1. Cut a piece of card. The width of the card is cut as long as the tassle length required. The length of the card is cut three times longer than the width.
2. Lay a piece of thread along the length of the card.
3. Closely wrap the card with the wool or thread
4. Securely tie the original piece of thread that you lay down.
5. Wrap the neck of the tassel with yarn and end off securely. The yarn used to wrap can be the same yarn as the tassel or it may be a contrast.
6. Cut the loops off the wrapped threads at the bottom of the tassel.

SPECIAL EFFECTS

- Use different threads and colours to wrap around the cardboard and create the tassel.
- Decorate the head of the tassel with beads.
- Crochet a "cap" for the head of the tassel.
- For a glitsy effect add some metallic threads when wrapping the tassel.

Bought tassels can be expensive and relatively uninteresting compared with ones that can be made. Add a personal touch to the garment in this way.

4.

5.

6.

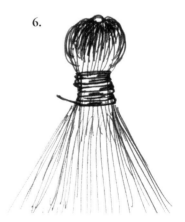

Shisha Mirrors

This type of embroidery was done traditionally in India and has since been adopted by many cultures and artists because of its wonderful exotic nature. Traditionally these mirrors were used with bright colours symbolising birth, youth, ageing and death. This embroidery is still used extensively in embellishing garments, book covers and bed covers.

The materials used when applying these mirrors should be firm enough to cope with the weight of the mirrors and thread. Closely woven cottons and linens work well. Avoid using thin fabrics or those that stretch too much. Pre-wash fabrics before using them. Chain, ladder, stem, buttonhole and backstitch are the most commonly used stitches together with the Shisha mirrors.

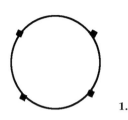

1.

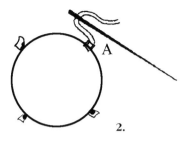

2.

ATTACHING SHISHA MIRRORS

1. Using a little fabric glue secure the mirror in place. This just makes the whole process easier. One doesn't have to use glue. Mark 4 points around the mirror. i.e. the corners of a square.
2. Thread a needle with thread and bring it up at point A.
3. Take the thread across the surface of the mirror and down through the fabric at point B. making a small stitch.
4. Bring the thread up at B and insert it at C. Catch a stitch and come up below this point.
5. Bring the thread up at C and insert the needle at D.
6. Bring the needle back at point D and down at A. Anchor the thread firmly at the back. (One can work an optional extra square in order to secure the mirror even further as shown in figure 6b)
7. Once the mirror is anchored with this network of stitches, work a circle of buttonhole around the mirror.
8. Starting at C work a stitch under the square base of stitches catching the fabric around the mirror each time.
9. Continue working around the mirror. The direction of the stitches must always radiate outwards. Work until the circle is complete.

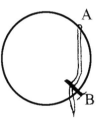

3.

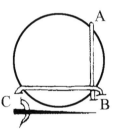

4.

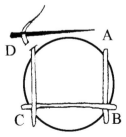

5.

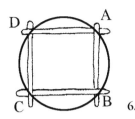

6.

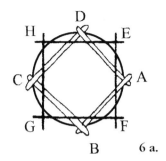

6 a.

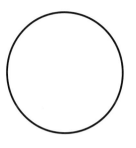

1. Glue mirror in place

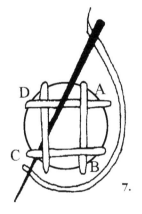

7.

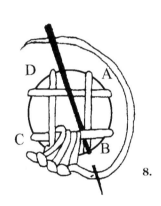

8.

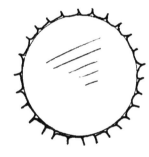

2. Work a row of buttonhole stitch the whole way around it.

Shisha mirror completely attached

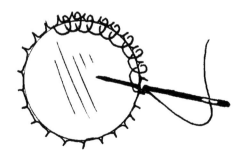

3. Work the next row of buttonhole on the previous row – working inwards and so trapping the mirror. 2, 3 or 4 rows of buttonhole stitch can be worked.

Quilting

Quilting is the stitching together of three layers of fabric to create the fabric sandwich. This will give your garment a three dimensional, padded look.

The choice of batting is extremely important for a garment as opposed to a quilt. The batting for a garment needs to be flexible and have the ability to mould to the body. It should also have weight in order to allow the garment to hang well. It is sometimes advisable to use a heavyweight fabric as a batting when one doesn't want a bulky look. Be aware when buying batting that it is of a bonded type, as fibres of non bonded battings will often migrate through the surface of the fabric. It can be very disappointing to have the garment come alive with lots of little migrating fibres all over a garment that you have spent hours working on. I like to work with 100% cotton batting made by Fairfield Processing in America. They have various weights of battings made of both synthetic and natural fibres.

Most garments need an area of quiet and quilting can create this effect if worked in an area in a simple way. Quilting also creates wonderful texture. These textured areas often offset and enhance areas of extreme busyness.

The most important thing to remember with quilting is that you must baste the layers together properly. This will prevent Puckering. There are numerous ways to baste a quilt, the most common being that of using long basting stitches. I find this time consuming and not always fool-proof. I am going to explain the way that I find the easiest. With this method, I use safety pins.

BASTING

Using masking tape, tape the backing fabric to a smooth tiled floor, with the right side facing the floor. The fabric must be pulled tight when taped.

Lay the batting on top of your backing fabric. This need not be pulled tight, but must be smoothed until flat.

Place the top layer over these 2 layers, right side up. Make sure that it is also lying flat.

Starting in the very centre and using 1 inch safety pins, pin the three layers together. Pins should be placed at intervals of about a fist apart. Smooth the top layer and make absolutely sure that it is flat as you work.

Once the whole surface has been pinned, close all the safety pins, remove the masking tape and you are ready to quilt.

I find this method of basting fool-proof as the back is so tightly anchored to the floor with tape that it cannot move and one only has to worry about getting the top surface smooth. I very rarely have to deal with puckers while quilting and if I do have excess fabric then all I do is move a pin slightly and continue quilting.

THE QUILT SANDWICH

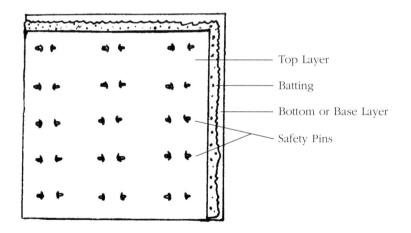

Top Layer

Batting

Bottom or Base Layer

Safety Pins

MACHINE QUILTING

Some machines have a special quilting foot which helps move the 3 layers of fabric through at an even pace. This is not necessary however, as your ordinary foot can be used for straight-line quilting as well as a darning foot when doing free machine quilting.

For straight quilting set the machine on a stitch length of 3. For free quilting, drop the feed dog and set the stitch length on 0. Remember to keep a steady pressure on the foot peddle and keep your hands moving at an even pace feeding the fabric under your foot. It is best to baste a small practise piece of fabric and master this free style quilting technique before starting on a precious garment. The old saying of "practise makes perfect" definitely applies here.

When beginning the stitching, bring the bobbin thread to the top surface and work 3 or 4 tiny stitches (stitch length 0). Now you can begin stitching. To end off your work, the same 3 or 4 stitches should be sewn. These cotton ends can be threaded back into the batting once the quilting has been completed and the ends are then cut off.

PROBLEM SOLVING

- If your garment is large and too cumbersome to fit under a machine try rolling it on each side, so that only the piece that you are quilting is flat under your machine.
- Place your machine on a large table so that it supports the garment.
- Remember to stop and relax your shoulders every now and again, as they can become quite stiff and sore.
- Beware of working some areas too intensely and others not, as this can cause waving and distortion and you will find that the garment will not lie flat or hang well.
- Hand quilting works well on traditional garments whereas machine quilting is suited to more contemporary garments.

SPECIAL EFFECTS

- Try using metallic thread. Loosen the top tension to prevent it from snapping.
- Work different quilting designs in different areas.
- Use a cordonet needle which is available at Bernina outlets.

HAND QUILTING

Hand quilting is the process by which the three layers of fabric in the quilt sandwich are stitched together with evenly spaced and sized running stitches. To make the running stitches weave the needle in and out of the three layers using a rocking motion. To begin, make a knot in the thread and pull it through the top layer into the batting. To end off use the same process. Any visible thread ends should then be cut off level with the fabric.

When quilting choose a strong sewing thread or quilting thread which is available from most quilt stores. The needle should be short and fine.

Rolling the quilt sandwich thus allowing it to fit under the machine arm.

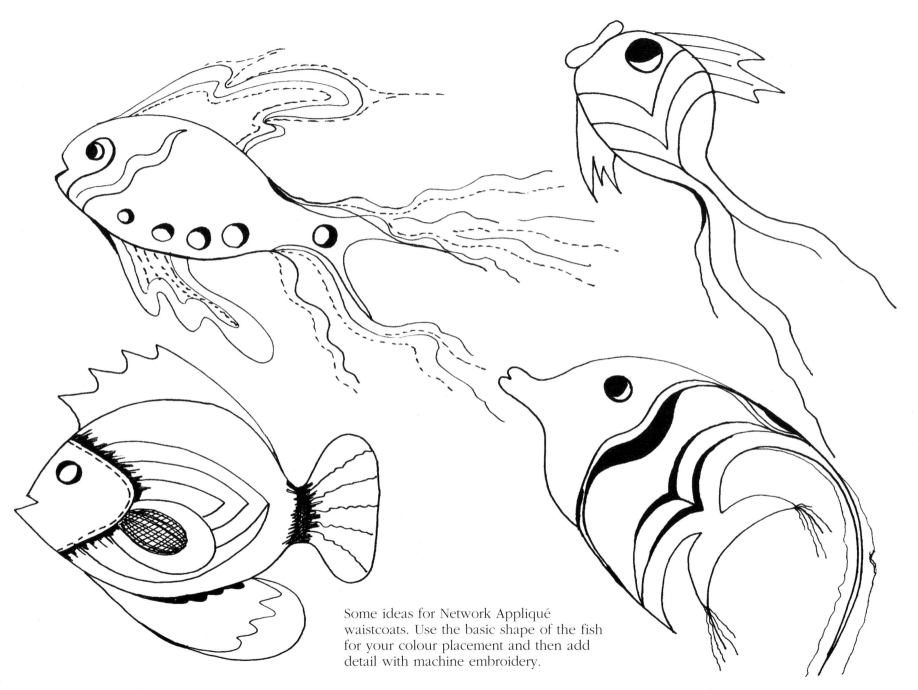

Some ideas for Network Appliqué
waistcoats. Use the basic shape of the fish
for your colour placement and then add
detail with machine embroidery.